READING SIMULACRA

THE SUNY SERIES IN
POSTMODERN CULTURE
Joseph Natoli, editor

READING
SIMULACRA

**Fatal Theories
for Postmodernity**

M. W. Smith

State University of New York Press

Cover image: Corbis Images

Published by
State University of New York Press, Albany

© 2001 State University of New York

All rights reserved

Printed in the United States of America

No part of this book may be used or reproduced in any manner whatsoever without written permission. No part of this book may be stored in a retrieval system or transmitted in any form or by any means including electronic, electrostatic, magnetic tape, mechanical, photocopying, recording, or otherwise without the prior permission in writing of the publisher.

For information, address State University of New York Press,
90 State Street, Suite 700, Albany, NY 12207

Production by Judith Block
Marketing by Michael Campochiaro

Library of Congress Cataloging-in-Publication Data

Smith, M. W. (Michael W.), 1963-
    Reading simulacra : fatal theories for postmodernity / M.W. Smith.
        p. cm. -- (SUNY series in postmodern culture)
    Includes bibliographical references and index.
    ISBN 0-7914-5063-5 (alk. paper) -- ISBN 0-7914-5064-3 (pbk. : alk. paper)
    1. Postmodernism. 2. Reality. 3. Subjectivity. 4. Subjectivity in literature. 5. Simulation methods--Social aspects. 6. Baudrillard, Jean. I. Title. II. Series.

HM449 .S553 2001
306'.01--dc21   00-066070

10 9 8 7 6 5 4 3 2 1

Contents

PREFACE	vii
ABBREVIATIONS	ix
INTRODUCTION	
Reading Simulacra: Toward a Bifocal Approach	1
CHAPTER 1	
Fatal Strategies	13
CHAPTER 2	
Nietzsche's Legacy: The Postmodern Will	29
CHAPTER 3	
Seduction, Radical Semiurgy, and the Logic of the Code	41
CHAPTER 4	
Technology and the (Dis)appearing Subject:	
Schizophrenia or Seduction?	65
CHAPTER 5	
Dehistoricized Subjectivity: Reese Williams and the Schizoid Text	77
CHAPTER 6	
Desire, Seduction, and Subjectivity in Kathy Acker's Novels:	
Blood and Guts in High School and *Don Quixote*	85
CHAPTER 7	
Clarence Major's *My Amputations*:	
African American Identity and Simulacra	103
CHAPTER 8	
Baudrillard's *America*:	
The Perfect Postmodern Object of Simulation	113
CHAPTER 9	
Media Culture on the Verge of Drama: Hyperreal O.J.	
and Simulacra in Oliver Stone's *Natural Born Killers*	119
NOTES	129
BIBLIOGRAPHY	133
INDEX	137

Preface

When *reading* the texts of postmodern culture one must accept the fact that postmodern experience is simulated experience, commonly called "simulacrum." Twentieth-century advancements in technology and information processing have brought about a new social order in which simulations and models interpenetrate our experiences of the world so deeply that the difference between reality and appearance evaporates. One could say, in other words, that now "the real" appears as simulation—and that this is occurring everywhere from the quantum level to the social. Computer-processed quantum probabilities project precisely onto reality, and DNA codes alone are used to issue arrest warrants for otherwise "unidentifiable" subjects. In a similar fashion, polls model our thinking and predict the outcome for us, so that social and political events seem to occur as destiny. Furthermore, a "visit" to Africa may appear more "genuine" at its virtual locations—Lion Country Safari, African Tours Ltd.'s home page, or on the TV documentary—than during the "real" trip to Kenya. Finally, fighter pilots (e.g., take the Gulf War) are "virtually" guided by digital programming networks, and the "field of operations" takes place, literally, on a computer monitor, making theorists such as Jean Bauldrillard posit that the Gulf War never "really" happened.

Much of recent theory addresses the connections among the residual categories of history, identity, reality, and representation in an age of simulation, and explores the "fatal" relations now between images and objects (including the body, written and screenal texts, and the social). This project is guided by a concern for the implications of Jean Baudrillard's work for human experience as it rapidly disappears into a high-tech, mass-media, "hyperreal" environment. Are we to accept Baudrillard's refusal of the autonomous historical subject—or the "always already" of postmodern subjectivity—implying our enclosure within a self-referential fun house of simulacra brought about by technological and informational hypertrophy, among other forces? If so, what sort of critique can be launched from within such a system? What new communication strategies have developed that might allow postmodern literature and culture to be "read" in our hyperreal epoch? Finally, what other accounts of postmodernism should we attend to in light of Baudrillard's wholesale denial of any stable connection between reality and representation? Regarding these questions, I examine figurations of Friedrich Nietzsche in recent theorists such as Jean Bauldrillard, Giles Deleuze and Felix Guattari, and Arthur and Marilouise Kroker in an effort to discern a bifocal method for "reading" the postmodern works under analysis in *Reading Simulacra: Fatal Theories for Postmodernity*. It is my belief that such a method is required as a means of surviving the postmodern scene.

I wish to thank S. E. Gontarski, Karen Cunningham, and Ralph Berry at Florida State University for their support of this project. Also, a special thank-you to Hope Kurtz and E. F. Kaelin for their editorial assistance in preparing the original manuscript. Finally, I am beholden to Joseph Natoli and to my editor at State University of New York Press, James Peltz, for his diligence in seeing this book through to publication.

Abbreviations

The most frequently cited works are indicated by the following abbreviations:

Kathy Acker
DQ   Don Quixote
B&GHS   Blood and Guts in High School

Jean Baudrillard
BL   Baudrillard Live: Selected Interviews
EC   The Ecstacy of Communication
EDOI   The Evil Demon Of Images
FS   Fatal Strategies
SE&D   Symbolic Exchange and Death
SED   Seduction
SIM   Simulations
SW   Selected Writings

Critical Art Ensemble
ED   The Electronic Disturbance

Giles Deleuze and Felix Guattari
AO   Anti-Oedipus
TP   A Thousand Plateaus

Jacques Derrida
EOO   The Ear of the Other
OG   Of Grammatology

Michel Foucault
LCP   Language, Counter-memory, Practice
M&C   Madness and Civilization
OT   The Order of Things

Arthur Kroker
BI *Body Invaders*
PI *The Possessed Individual*
PS *The Postmodern Scene*

Friedrich Nietzsche
GS *The Gay Science*
WP *The Will To Power*

Richard Rorty
CP *Consequences of Pragmatism*
RP "Feminism and Pragmatism" in *Radical Philosophy*

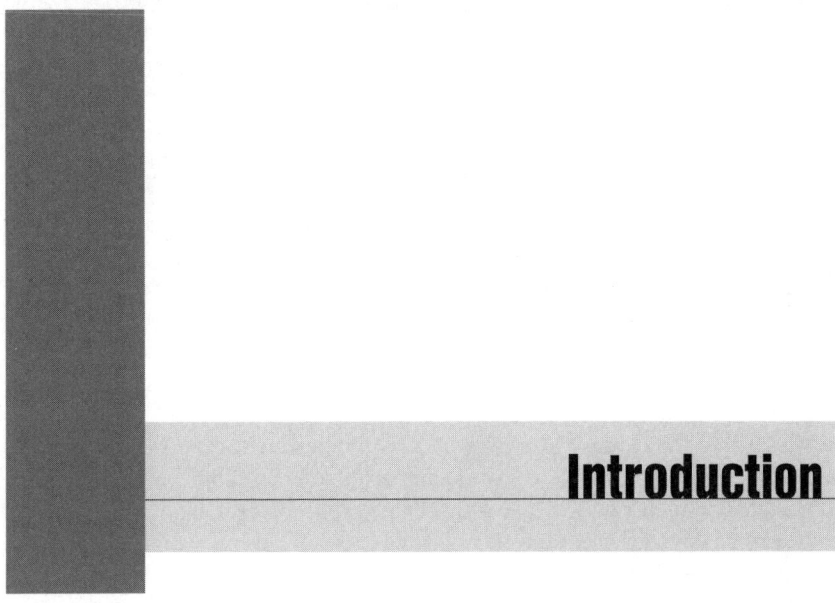

Introduction

READING SIMULACRA: TOWARD A BIFOCAL APPROACH

> Everything is destined to reappear as simulation. Landscapes as photography, women as the sexual scenerio, thoughts as writing, terrorism as fashion and the media, events as television. Things seem only to exist by virtue of this strange destiny. You wonder whether the world itself isn't just here to serve as advertising copy in some other world.
>
> —Jean Baudrillard, *America*

Postmodernity, fraught with computer simulations and screenally produced images, is often charged with giving up on reality and leaving us awash in computer-generated and media-constructed hyperreal. Oddly enough, in a world of simulation, appearances seem "more real" than the world of people and objects. This is the condition of hyperreality, in which reality is modeled on images. For today's "Generation Ne(x)t" reality is seemingly composed of an endless reduplication of signs—witness the image-producing machinery (advertising) of the fashion and cosmetic industries at work as it so readily slides from the television or print medium onto living human beings in the clothing they wear and lifestyles they portray. At this point, the real slides into, becomes indistinguishable from the hyperreal product of media images, models, memory banks, and statistical outcomes, from which it can be reproduced indefinitely (*SIM* 3). Everywhere around us the real is being (re)produced and (re)processed as simulation—from compact disc music, which digitalizes an analogue model for sound, to cybersex (an interpersonal experience in the form of an electronic transmission), to virtual visitation and voyeur programs that allow us to "be" anywhere in the world via computer uplinks. Stephen Pfohl calls this the "ultramodern technological absorption of what's real into what's simulated" (66). Furthermore, the circulation of images of "the real" through television advertising, and other screenal forms such as computers serves to erase any sense of a "real" beneath the image. In fact, the real is now defined and delineated as that which can be represented or reproduced through these technological forms (*SE&D* 73). Consider for a moment "real TV" or the way in which there no longer seems to be any distinction between "real life" and television, especially when real life is increasingly becoming the subject of TV in broadcasts such as *Cops*, *The Real World*, the Gulf War saga, and the O. J. Simpson trial. One might question if television still serves as merely a representation of life or if some strange reversal has taken place akin to that of Thomas Pynchon's *Vineland* in which the Thanatoids and other characters "live out" TV representations? Don't forget to bring your camcorder with you everywhere, since you never know when "real TV" might happen.

In *The Evil Demon of Images*, Baudrillard says that the phenomenon of simulacrum is a fatal implosion of the image with the real, and that the resultant "hyperreal" overcoding of the real by the processed image allows appearances to become reality. That is, in the topos of simulacra, any distinction between the represented image and reality vanishes as the historical contexts in which images were produced are effaced by their (re)production and circulation. Finally all determinate processes are overthrown and recuperated by the indeterminacy of the late-capitalist code (*SE&D* 7). Baudrillard describes the process:

> For some time now, in the dialectical relationship between reality and images (that is, the relation that we wish to believe dialectical, readable from the real to the image and vice versa), the image has taken over and imposed its own immanent ephemeral logic; an immoral logic without depth, beyond good and evil, beyond truth and falsity; a logic of the extermination of its own referent, a logic of the implosion of meaning in which the message disappears on the horizon of the medium. (*SE&D* 23)

It's the tail wagging the dog.

In postmodern simulacra, the contents of messages (their use value as information) are determined by their forms (their exchange value as media). Media always find themselves referring back to their currency (their exchange value as images) within the channels of media themselves (Beller note 25).

Hypermedia and the technological proliferation of information have so blurred the differences between images and their referents that on today's "planet Hollywood," images often refer back only to other images as their origin of reference and no longer to anything "real." As all referentials are liquidated in the field of visual circulation, the context and conditions of historical production simply no longer matter. It becomes specifically the circulation within the medium that matters in this abstract system. Use values (contents of a message) are then erased in favor of exchange values (currency as images) and the "medium becomes the message." [1] According to Baudrillard, the apotheosis of medium = message is reached in public opinion polls that in fact serve not simply to produce a reality or signification—a mere simulation according to the mode of questioning, or model set up to privilege particular variables—but to reproduce the simulacrum of public opinion (a perpetual representation of its own image). Thus the public opinion poll, itself, serves as evidence that there is public opinion (*SE&D* 65-66). For Baudrillard, it's this "cool" circulation of signs, words, and images-as-commodities that creates the logic of the late-capitalist consumer code.

Baudrillard's views are contested, however, by Marxist critics for whom his brand of postmodernism is "hopelessly enmeshed" within the "late-capitalist nightmare of high-tech, mass marketing, and consumption" (Hutcheon and Natoli 301). As one account among many, his is criticized by some for "giving up on reality." According to the view presented by Linda Hutcheon, and Joseph Natoli in *A Postmodern Reader:* "The reflexivity that we have seen as characterizing the postmodern in this view, however, can actually uncover nothing: the postmodern clash of representations is already 'enveloped' by what Baudrillard calls 'simulation.' The plurality of narratives, of representations, and of the 'real,' is here reduced to a monist 'Hyperreality' in which all connections are 'unhinged'" (306). The problem for Marxist critics lies in the indeterminacy of postmodern assertions that totalizing narratives, truth claims, and even the real or historical world, are all swept away in a monistic signifying system of late-capitalist consumer ideology (à la structuralism), suggesting a social structure of surface without depth, and, thus, disallowing for the possibility of dialectical critique—which is to see society as a big sign system that refuses the privileged position of politics or history. As Christopher Norris puts it, Baudrillard "assumes that 'reality' is structured through and through by the order of signs or symbolic equivalences; that our knowledge of the world can amount to nothing more than our mode of insertion into this all-encompassing economy of signs; and thus that any attempt to distinguish 'real' needs or use-values from their order of 'imaginary' representation is necessarily a vain effort and chimerical delusion" (188). For many contemporary theorists (Marxist, poststructural, and feminist alike) interested in issues of representation, history, and subjectivity, Baudrillard's antirealist doctrine, or "logic of the simulacrum," presents a difficult impasse. However, to postmodern critics such as Arthur

Kroker, Baudrillard's schematic (drawn from the Saussurian paradigm) serves to resituate the critique of representation in terms of its relation to reality, not merely to efface all determinate connections between the two. Still, it is shown in the writing of Mike Gane, that Baudrillard's own early efforts to develop Marxism failed on this very account. [2] To fully understand Baudrillard's "fatal" account of representation, it is necessary to return to the writing of Friedrich Nietzsche, from whom the (post)structuralist critique of representation—especially in the work of Jacques Derrida (logocentricism) and Michel Foucault (subjectivity and power/knowledge)—has followed (chapter 1).

The correlation of Nietzsche and Baudrillard (chapter 2) is well developed in the work of Kroker, especially in *The Possessed Individual* and in *The Postmodern Scene*, in which he and David Cook discern that postmodern nihilism has clearly been the trajectory of Western consciousness since the Enlightenment. Nietzsche, who proclaimed the next two hundred years as his legacy, foresaw that the forces of the classical episteme—representational thought—and the eventual formation of the bourgeois individual would "disenchant" human existence and result in a modern paradigm shift [3] that he warned would end in "nihilism." In this new order of things, which is just now beginning to be fully realized, our cosmological relation to divinity and myth would be replaced with our status as individual consumers caught within market relations (late-capitalist code). It is prophetic that in *The Gay Science*, the Madman goes to the marketplace to proclaim that "God is dead." In postmodern nihilism, driven by the power of the dollar sign ($) and by the image-commodity, consumption is the very purpose of life. As one company tells us: "Life's a Sport—Drink It Up!" Our postmodern culture is saturated with commodity signification (clothes as signs of wealth, soft drinks as signs of youth, and cars as signs of status). In this pervasive consumer culture, where individuals "will to signify" (and anything is possible; just turn on the TV), Nietzsche's belief in the art of "self-creation" is dead, having been replaced by empty prepackaged computer profiles of our every desire.

As a nineteenth-century philologist, Nietzsche understood the metaphoric system of "fatal" exchanges at the thrust of Western thought: sign for referent, absence for presence, representation for real, same for difference, perspective for truth, and science and material wealth for God. These reversals, or "fatal strategies," are reaching their apogee in postmodernity, where life (as will) takes on a completely semiological complexion, and reality implodes in the nihilistic logic of the image, or technologically induced sign. That is, Western culture now operates under a semiurgical "image-system" that serves as the basis of social exchange in which signs replace referents and images replace objects in the circulation of consumer code to which reality conforms. In this light, reality serves as a "site of exterminism" in radical semiurgy, wherein the modern "will" reverses the real into image, across what Kroker calls "the landscape of the power/sign" (*PS* 33). Kroker and Cook point out: "All along, the 'will to power' had never been anything more than a brilliant inferno for the liquidation of the 'real' and for the processing of society into the dark seductive empire of the sign" (*PS* 33). Kroker adduces:

> For Nietzsche, what powered this fantastic reduction of society to the logic of the sign, what precipitated the implosion of the real into the semiology of perspectival illusion, was this: *the sign is power on its down side, on its side of reversal, cancellation, and disaccumulation. The Will to Power* is the emblematic text which represents, at once, the locus and limit of the postmodernist imagination, or what is the same, the tragic theory of the sign which is everywhere now in political discourse. Nietzsche recognized that the sovereignty of the sign (he described sign-systems in the language of "perspectival valuations") meant the final reduction of society (abstract, semiological, and structural) to the language of willing [italics mine]. (*PS* 33)

Nietzsche easily understood the disappearance of the real into the locus of abstract power (signs) because it was nothing new. For some time now, power has relied on its absence, its ability to disappear, or transfigure into a sign.

Robert Marin's study, *Portrait of the King*, explains how Louis XIV employed an abstract (or symbolic) exchange of power by having his portrait painted, extending the dominion of power throughout the state as a function of image (xii). In this case: "The king's body can be refracted everywhere throughout the state, as a fragmentary presence... [his] means of control are not those of a repressive agency, but rather as multifariously autonomous but homologous styles of aura" (xii). Similarly "ghostly" [4] effects of representational power haunt us everywhere today, while greatly decentralized and disseminated in myriad means of official simulation, including media, advertising, and other areas of mass communications through which "subjectivity" is produced. Many theorists point out that simulation has always taken place in the Western tradition; the postmodern displacement of the real by the televisual image, advertising sign, or computer model is merely the current incarnation. Plato's [5] writings express the conviction that true referents of words are not in the world of reality, but exist in a realm of ideas or forms so that the real, itself, follows up the idea, or form, as a simulation. Our present mass-media culture marks a radical shift, however, wherein the simulation industry has the capacity to seize on and "copy," again, all of reality, making the simulacra function and positing the world as a phantasm.

The ubiquitous effects of today's ritualistic high-velocity technological and media "processing" of all spheres of "reality" have been called "vertiginous" by postmodern philosophers such as Fredric Jameson. [6] What results is a hyperreal culture of pastiche and reprocessed images and texts from the past. Furthermore, the speed at which history and culture are reduplicated leaves us with no grounding, no reference point, no origin for judging what is real, and no finite or objective perspective, only simulacra. [7] In these simulacra, the present suffers from a colonization of images and texts of the past. For example, long after their "corporeal" deaths, Elvis is everywhere; Charlie Chaplan sells computers; and Fred Astaire dances with Paula Abdul in Pepsi commercials. Without an origin of difference, implosion of a sense of history is experienced wherein the past and present are undifferentiated. The result is cultural schizophrenia acquired from the endless flow of signs and reproduced images that leads to a loss of stable meaning. At the heart of the discussion is this issue: If, as Nietzsche and Derrida espouse, "meaning" emanates from *difference*, what happens as difference is erased by the fatal strategies of the postmodern sign (indeterminacy of the code), where, in simulacra, there is no distinguishable difference between representation and real, image and object, past and present? As one response, the nomadic thought of Giles Deleuze and Felix Guattari attempts to "ride difference." Nomadic thought does not respect the artificial divisions between representation, subjectivity, and being, instead replacing them with a conductivity without bounds (Massumi 5).

Nietzsche felt that human (totalizing) systems stress "being" over "becoming" (*Zarathustra* 113), or "same" over "difference" and "simulation" over "the real." Nietzsche claims: "We have projected the conditions of our preservation as predicates of being in general. Because we have to be stable in our beliefs if we are to prosper, we have made the 'real' world a world not of change and *becoming*, but one of being" [italics mine] (*WP* 276). Following from Nietzsche's description of an impending modernization, we suddenly find ourselves in a dangerous state of reversals (fashion for identity, sign for real, and image for everything) where theories of "being" replace "becoming" in a tragic vision of human existence. In that light, what can be said of *reading*, when it, like everything else, carries the inscription of the "always already?" That is, what does it mean to "read" the simulacrum of postmodernity, where *reading* may be no less than selective decoding of late-capitalist image-producing machinery, or, its opposite, where to interpret is to metatheorize to such an extent that all experience is transformed into fatal strategies of existence (another form of simulacrum)?

Through a bifocal approach that encompasses Baudrillard (chapter 3) and Deleuze and Guattari (chapter 4) it is possible to "read" simulacra as "fatal strategies" that erase differences in the production of desire and in the processing of cultural texts (information, mass media, and advertising) for consumption in late-capitalist consumer culture. For example, through the power of mass media (mis)representation and simulated consensus (opinion polls, testimonial commercials, etc.), there no longer appears to be any gap between what people want and what is promised (manufactured totally within this feedback system) (Norris 42). Where referentiality is suspended, it is no longer possible to distinguish model from reality or simulation from its source. In a world in which signs only refer to other signs, *seduction*, which plays only in appearances, is an operative model for reality. Affirming the play of empty signifiers, Baudrillard concedes to a strategy of seduction: "Seduction as an invention of stratagems, of the body, as a disguise for survival . . . as a dissuasion which is stronger yet than that of the system" (*EC* 74-75). In seduction, the advantage of the object (body, commodity, work of art, etc.) lies in the fact that it always already exists as it is defined by the late-capitalist culture. The object-image is simultaneously commodity and currency in circulation within the self-referential operations of the consumer code. Baudrillard privileges the logic of the object that defies the subject by an indifference to desire: "The object is without desire, it is that which escapes desire and belongs to the order of destiny" (*SW* 52). In a neutral world of simulation (destiny as opposed to desire): "The object can resist through oversimulation, hypersimulation, infantilism, total dependence" (Gane 197).

Whereas Baudrillard proposes the alternative of seduction and "'resistance-as-object' (*PS* 176) as the line of political resistance most appropriate to the simulacrum" (Kroker and Levin 133), reaffirming desire-as-production, Deleuze and Guattari propose the "schizoid" subject as a means of rupture. The "schizophrenic" response to "subjectivity" is a rhizomatic (or diffuse) resistance that subsumes the subject/object dichotomy. The connection of the sign to the object (routed through desire) can be broken through rhizomatic maneuvering of the subject becoming a "body without organs" (BwO). Brian Massumi says to "think of the body without organs as the body outside any determinate state, poised for any action in its repertory" (70). To make yourself a body without organs, Deleuze and Guattari say:

> Lodge yourself on a stratum, experiment with the opportunities it offers, find an advantageous place on it, find potential movements of deterritorialization, possible lines of flight, experience them, produce flow conjunctions here and there, try out continuums of intensities segment by segment . . . It is through meticulous relation with the strata that one succeeds in freeing the lines of flight, causing conjugated flows to pass and escape and bringing forth continuous intensities for a BwO. Connect, conjugate, continue: a whole "diagram," as opposed to still signifying and subjective formations. (*A Thousand Plateaus* 161)

This produces a transformational potential for social and self "becoming." In postmodernity, however, this force tends to be toward "becoming-consumer" (136).

Baudrillard and Deleuze and Guattari all assume the present dissolution of the representational subject able to provide a vantage point on reality (*SW* 6), which leads to a cultural schizophrenia in which the subject can no longer delineate the limits of her own being apart from the networks of capitalist code (*EC* 27). For, within these networks, desire appears everywhere as simulation. The terrorism of simulacra is the destiny of "desire" as circulated code, where the sign/image replaces the object (its referent) in this coding. The image is commodity; and individuals, as "desiring machines," are sites that process the coded messages of (empty) consumption. In resistance, a rhizomatic strategy pursues the production of desire to the edge and then submerges into the cultural sign system so as not to shut itself off. Deleuze and Guattari's *Anti-Oedipus* calls for subjective multiplicity, difference, nomadology, de-individualization, and displaced desire (do not allow it to be represented—let it become). Their "schizophrenia" is a positive process of Nietzschean self-invention, connection, and expansion, "an enlargement of life's limits" across capital relations (Massumi 1). Instead of suppression, free political action and a proliferation of desires are gained by lines of flight through an "anti-Oedipal" working against the subjective fascism of the state apparatuses of late-capitalism: consumerism, the media, religious and political ideologies, and so forth.

Thus, I offer a critical comparison of two seemingly polemical methods imbued with Nietzschean philosophy for reading postmodern simulacra (the objects, texts, and artifacts of postmodernity). One can read postmodern simulacra as an "implosion"—stressing uncertainty and seduction—as do Baudrillard and Kroker, or its apparent opposite, as "rupture"—stressing multiple desires and rhizomatic becomings—as do Deleuze and Guattari. In Baudrillard's signifying equation, all signs level out in an inexorable sign slide (the implosion of meaning) toward indifference and substitution. Here, the operations of late-capitalism appear as a "shimmering metonymic surface" as Massummi puts it (45). At this point, seduction becomes "surrendering oneself to the allure of the sign" (178). As opposed to this logic, which Massumi says "fails to go off on a tangent" (179) and merely succumbs to the circular logic of consumerism, Deleuze and Guattari offer a postmodern strategy of schizophrenic play and experimentation—a sign slide of potentiality and becoming both through a horizontal flow of signs (language) and the vertical actualization of molecular transformations amid capital relations (the subject's identity axis intersecting with ideological codes—especially that of consumerism). Realized in this motion is the BwO's unfolding in space and time: "What Deleuze and Guattari are after is a real perception of the superhuman 'becoming' immanent to human being, a pragmatic embrace of meaning in its infinite but fractional dimensionality" (45).

The difference in subjective and objective strategies notwithstanding, Deleuze and Guattari might yet find a place in the hyperreal topography of Baudrillard. The distinguishing factor setting them apart is that the latter sees this societal leveling of images (simulation) as producing an undimensional subjectivity that is fatal, whereas the former looks toward simulation's "mutational aptitude" and the potential for "becoming" that it allows. "Becoming-molar" is itself always already a form of simulation: "persons are simulacra derived from a social aggregate whose code is invested for its own sake" (*AO* 366). It follows, reasons Massumi, that "[t]he images so ubiquitous in the urban landscape are nothing less than commodified transformational matrices in an escape run from molarity" (135). In this universe, the referent doesn't lose out to the image because the referent (or the signifier, for that matter) was never in the realm of "vertical content" anyhow (Massumi 45)—content is always only realized in the force of "becoming." And "becoming other" is found in potential force between the molecular and the molar—never caught in Being, but a simulation that "overthrows the model once and for all" (181). The only drawback, that is, if you wish to make it that, is that the "posthuman" condition is a "becoming" that is "fundamentally a becoming consumer" where our "transformational potential tends to be restricted to image-consumption and -production" (136). An individual's existence in this new "shop 'til you drop image universe" is controlled only by the limit on her credit cards. If you sport a Gold Visa, you can even redefine your gender if you wish—at the local gender market, buy an organ transplant package including facial hair removal and hormone shots, complete with lipstick and makeup for the final touches. In the capitalist and consumerist axiomatic of Barbara Kruger: "I buy, therefore, I am."

Here, one confronts Nietzsche's "last Man," who must "will to will." Nietzsche's "will to will" is phrased by Kroker in Heideggerian terms as a metamorphosis in the life order that replaces a ground in sensuous existence with an abstract and symbolic logic of human agency that will finally play itself out in technology (*PS* 223). He calls the "will to will" a "semiological unity imposed on an order of experience which was always only a system of mirroring affects" (*PS* 34). In poststructural terms, the "will to will" could be seen as spawned from the endemic "lack" or "play" of language, without origin or finitude, which the human linguistic experience "traces" ad infinitum (as a form of [re]production). Most importantly, the postmodern will is operative fully within the consumer code, where the subject must will incessantly for more code. Here, "desire," as will, is produced by the code and circulates as a simulacrum. In this process the "will" is nothing but the will to simulation, wherein subjects must "will to will" just to continue to exist. How appropriate: A "yuppie" drives a new Lexus car with "DUNLIVN" on the tags. If, according to the consumer code, materially defined happiness were ever fully acquired in the sign, the final exchange could only be with death.

At this fatal site of cultural simulations the coding of ideological meanings is brought to the level of personal experience, often garnering unfulfilled images of pleasure to those marginalized selves who either can't afford or fail to "fit the image," or creating images of difference by which to define these social groups as Other. Do a majority of African American smokers smoke menthol cigarettes because they taste better, or is it because "blacks" are the imagined target market? Furthermore, how does the buying and consumption of Cool cigarettes economically/socially code an individual as opposed to a Marlboro or Camel smoker? Massumi asserts: "Media, marketing, and advertising are mechanisms for abstracting and commercializing codes of human identity and their molecular components" (134). In this image-based economy, the postmodern subject assumes its identity and unfolds its life "along the lines laid down by the code enveloped in its images" (134). Here, human existence hyperdrives into a virtual dimension in which our entire molecular makeup has been capitalized. That is: "Gender, race, ethnicity, religious practices, belief systems, beauty, health, leisure—and every other aspect of molar human existence—has been resolved into component parts—images that may be purchased by a body and self-applied as desired" (135). As Massumi says: "It used to be that assuming or redefining an identity took a lifetime. Now it can be done in as long as it takes to shop for an image" (134).

Ultimately, is it possible to deterritorialize the localized structures of simulacra that produce contemporary desires (Deleuze and Guattari); or is it the destiny of signs to enter the dark abyss of seduction and become the simulacra of overdetermined subjectivity, meaning, and interpretation (Baudrillard)? From both vantage points, postmodern writing is seen as, itself, a culturally material practice, participating in the network of production and consumption of commodified simulacra: "truth," "history," "self," "reality" "identity," "body," and "America"—all doubled under the cynical sign of postmodern power (consumerism, capitalism, nihilism, etc.).

This project thus proceeds by questioning what it means to be human when these foundational categories of "meaning" appear as simulacra, and every act of "reading" (interpreting) is always already a fatal return. Both the artists and theorists included here—like the media, the institutions, the masses themselves—operate within the scene of a hyperreality. Yet, these writers and the cultural artifacts they produce pose questions to readers of how one is to proceed in the obscenity of a hypersignified existence so as to read the fatal texts of postmodernity. How is one to consider *reading* the textual object, when the process of doing so may result in the "parasiting" (ritually performing according to the dominant code) of postmodernity, as Pfohl puts it in *Death at the Parasite Cafe*?

The work of Baudrillard and the Krokers could certainly be seen as the apogee to the metaphysical palimpsest of fatal theory. Theirs is hypertheory that speaks the decay of all the great signs ("history," "reality," "identity," "truth," etc.) as it maneuvers through the remnants of a catastrophe. These theorists invite the implosion of meaning by the fatal strategies that define the cynical postmodern epoch. The Krokers, in their *Panic Encyclopedia*, define one way of participating in these fatal strategies as "panic reading." Accordingly, in the introduction to the second edition of the *Postmodern Scene*, Kroker and David Cook set the "mood" for the *fin-de-millennium*:

> Refusing (with Nietzsche) the pragmatic compromise which seeks to preserve, *The Postmodern Scene* can recommend so enthusiastically panic reading because it seeks to relieve the gathering darkness by a new and more local, cultural strategy. That is, to theorize with such hyper-intensity that the simulacrum is forced finally to implode into the density of its own

detritus, and to write so faithfully under the schizoid sign of Nietzsche and Bataille that burnout, discharge, and waste as the characteristic qualities of the postmodern condition are compelled to reveal lingering traces on the after-images of (our) bodies, politics, sexuality, and economy. (ii)

Hence, this project, along with Kroker and Cook, moves past an aesthetic world into a postmodernist hyperaesthetics of immanent surface, and returns to appropriate the pessimistic sign of a fatal strategy first proclaimed by Nietzsche.

Like Kroker and Cook, I intend to follow the present trajectory of the individual into nihilistic, all-pervasive technological and media-saturated forms of experiencing life as it is represented in recent writing. Among other things, the postmodern works studied herein address the (dis)appearance of the "self" and the "body" into simulation models, lifestyle images, and media doubles. Norman K. Denzin writes: "The ingredients of the postmodern self are given in three key cultural identities, those . . . that define gender, social class, race and ethnicity. The patriarchal . . . cultures of the world ideologically code the self and its meaning in terms of the meanings brought to these three cultural identities" (viii). I have chosen to examine a number of contemporary texts which, by portraying just such simulacral forms of experience, are able to subvert conventional representations of human subjectivity. In Clarence Major's *My Amputations*, a media stereotyped African American identity is confronted by the main character in his genealogical quest. In Reese Williams' *A Pair of Eyes*, the reader-subject explores its historical and ideological overcoding by media representations. And in Kathy Acker's *Blood and Guts in High School*, and *Don Quixote*, those sights ("desire," "love," "the self," and "the body") coded by (His)tory, culture, and technology, are reappropriated offering alternative figurations of female subjectivity (subversive, nomadic, and multiple). According to Rosi Braidotti, such *"figuration* refers to a style of thought that evokes or expresses ways out of the phallocentric vision of the subject" (1). In part, all of these works express the inability of Other to experience the commodified pleasures that our consumer culture purports to provide: "The raw economic, racial, and sexual edges of contemporary life produce anxiety, alienation, a radical isolation from others, madness, violence, insanity. . . . They bear witness to an economy, a political ideology, and a popular culture which can never deliver the promised goods to their households" (Denzin viii). Reflecting cultural constructions, these politically informed texts may be read as fatal sites that are both transformative within, and resistive to, cultural simulacra.

Reading Simulacra, then, studies the maneuvers of these experimental literary texts that speak as points of rupture within the institutional lining of our culture: Williams' work implodes the historical and cultural production of codes and images (chapter 5); Acker's brand of "punk feminism" disrupts conventional pathworks of "desire" in the phallogocentric text (chapter 6); Major's postmodern writing style equates the simulacrum of identity with death (chapter 7), challenging the notions of an authentic and stereotypically reducible African American experience. Finally, America itself is the quintessential postmodern object (chapter 8)—a media culture so virtual that the commodification of lived events by television verge on drama, as witnessed in the O. J. Simpson trial and Oliver Stone's *Natural Born Killers* (chapter 9). In all, these works call for simulacra to usher forth new systems of meaning, new formulations of identity. Moreover, these forms of writing deterritorialize "desire," so as to create the (counter) production of codes, identity, and images by which these texts—as lines of flight—resist simulation in Western culture. I have chosen these marginal texts because, in Nietzschean fashion, they offer perspectival readings—that is, one can simultaneously read them from positions both of schizophrenia (Deleuze and Guattari) and seduction (Baudrillard).

It is the conviction of Kroker and Cook that as we enter a new millennium: "we are living in a waiting period [hyperinertia], a dead space, which will be marked by increasing and random outburst of political violence [drifts], schizoid behaviors [hypersubjectivity], and the implosion of all the signs of communication [hypersimulation] as western culture runs down towards the brilliant illumination of a final burnout" (*PS* vii). At this point *reading* is posed as a method of survival—not an "ethics," but a "method" based on various metaphors. One can "read" the simulacrum to "affirm" difference (Nietzsche's *becoming*); to "implode" meaning through seduction (Baudrillard's dark side); and to "rupture, multiply, schiz" (in the language of Deleuze and Guattari)—theoretical terms that reveal communication strategies designed for a world in which representation has collapsed.

Chapter One

Fatal Strategies

> Nihilism as a psychological state will have to be reached, *first*, when we have sought a "meaning" in all events that is not there: so the seeker eventually becomes discouraged. Nihilism, then, is the recognition of the long *waste* of strength, the agony of the "in vain," insecurity, the lack of any opportunity to recover and regain composure—being ashamed in front of oneself, as if one had *deceived* oneself all too long.
>
> —Nietzsche, *The Will to Power*

The crisis that confronts our triumphant will to culture is the crisis of representation, or the nihilistic foundation at the base of Western culture that finds its culmination in postmodern simulacra. As the site where the "postmodern critique of representation achieves its most searing expression" (*PS* 9), *The Will to Power* explains the fatal theory of Enlightenment thought that defines the domains of knowledge that miniaturize, categorize, and model the order of things. Without realizing it, humans have moved toward nihilism—killing Nature, God, Truth, and Self, by violently doubling them into the discourses of science, technology, information, and a telecommunicative imagery. Nietzsche, and later Michel Foucault, foresaw the fatality of objects whose destiny it is to disappear into a system of doubles, representation, or inscriptions: "[M]odern thought is one that moves no longer toward the never-completed formation of *Difference*, but towards the ever-to-be-accomplished unveiling of the Same. Now such an unveiling is not accomplished without the simultaneous appearance of *the Double*" [italics mine] (*OT* 340). Nietzsche summoned the individual who could overcome the fascist forms of semiurgical mastery, by which the "new" returns as the "same," which are imposed on the "becoming" by the aestheticization of everyday human experiences. Humanity might yet overcome this will to metaphor and simulation (today hyperrealized "within a technologically constructed matrix of aestheticized images" [Pfohl 35]) and recuperate seduction and gesture. For Jean Baudrillard, seduction is the "'form which remains to language when it has nothing more to say'" (qtd. in Morris 200). Nietzsche realized that human beings could never receive their destiny outside of language. All transference of human experience into language results in:

> Doublings that cut into and imprison the finite bodies of human animals made subject(s) to the power of abstracted linguistic logic; doublings that collectively impose artificial distortions in the process of translating the indeterminate cominglings of material relations-in-flux into the fixed and seemingly law-like rule of hierarchical binary condensations; doublings which sacrificially substitute the orderly reductions of signs or totems for the chaotic charms and playful intimacies of a multiplicity of ambivalent forms. (Pfohl 152)

Since G. W. F. Hegel, the struggle to realize a "nature" of humanity, apart from the institutions and customs that comprise the fabrication of history (its deterretorialization), has led to existential alienation and isolation of the individual into binary systems such as Subject/Object or Man/Nature. Today, the ever-accelerated historicization of humanity and its world into images within the dominion of a predominant technological narrative (dis)places the individual into relational matrices of technologies and ideologies of code, at the center of which lies its own disappearance.

Foucault's genealogy of "man," over the past one hundred and fifty years supports this concern: "As the archeology of our thought easily shows, man is an invention of recent date. And one perhaps nearing its end. If those arrangements were to disappear . . . then one can certainly wager that man would be erased, like a face drawn in sand at the edge of the sea" (*OT* 387). Foucault speculates that during the nineteenth century a caesura occurred that brought about an epoch when "words ceased to intersect with representations and to provide a spontaneous grid for the knowledge of things" (*OT* 304). At this same time, the human sciences appeared and the idea of "man" emerged as the focus of historical knowledge (*OT* 344). A proliferation of related discourses instituted themselves in many forms, predominantly in the natural sciences (and more so, today, in the social sciences). This discursive displacement of the space of "man" replaced it in discourse outside of itself, in a space "other" to itself, emptied of "truth." For example, one prevailing discourse, psychoanalytic theory, accompanied this idea of "man" the individual with that of the "Unconscious" (via Arthur Schopenhauer and Sigmund Freud). The Unconscious, an Other to the individual, is a silent but potentially talkative unthought; it is both external and internal, an indispensable but "obscure space." Jacques Lacan proposed that the "thinking of the unconscious, like that of the primitive man, is a functioning sign-system" (Harland 33): that is, the unconscious is structured like a language (*Ecrits* 234). This poststructuralist model of language brings with it the fatal aporias for the human of "the Other," the Real, the Lack, and Desire. The subject, "man," is as much an effect of unconscious desires as of conscious ones. The attempt to fill the space of the Unconscious, of Other, with language, instances one failure of the anthropocentric focus of knowledge because this attempt grants the Other (language, and metaphor) power. That is (symbolic) "representation" of the lack produces conditions for the sign-slide characterizing the Nietzschean world of "perspectival appearances"—the continual collapse of objective and subjective poles of experience (*PS* 93-94). The exchange between subject and object is described by Baudrillard as "redoubled simulation." According to Kroker: "A perfect refraction takes place in which the object viewed (signified) circles back and, in an instantaneous shift of perspective, becomes the locus . . . of signification itself" (*PS* 81). Ultimately, any concept of "man" (the subject) is consumed in the vacuum created by this transference of language and images to the "object."

With the disruption of the representational narrative that has dominated the past episteme, wherein a Cartesian dualistic linguistic model of the individual ("I think therefore I am") is transformed via the Enlightenment into the later positivist ideal ("I can represent the essence of myself"), "man" shifts from being a quintessential "subject" to being an object of metanarrative. (Nietzsche warned us of the loss of the "self" for a cynical world of pure "perspectival appearances.") René Descartes may well have been right, in a sense: language-thinking is the essence of humanity. But talking about that phenomenon—that is, placing it within a discursive field, where the individual is embodied in the linguistic fabric—creates the dualism that removes "man" from an understanding of self. As the discursive systems of the human sciences developed, "man," his social behavior, his psyche, and his body are defined (and moreover), created. Indeed, "man" has been subsumed into this grand narrative of representation. The objectification of "man" in discourse has created the phantom image; the signifier without a signified; the deterretorialization of self; in short, a manifold of simulacra. In its doubling, "man" becomes merely an image afloat in the linguistic field of natural sciences and, to a greater extent today, the social sciences, culminating in the loss of "self" in psychoanalytic theory, with the loss of "freedom" reduced to a function of the sign system (economic, political, class, etc.) in the modern productivist society of Marxist thought, a polemics in the gender issue, and ultimately a loss of "body" into the master narrative of the technocratic society (à la Jean-Francois Lyotard) and the simulacra of late capitalism (à la Deleuze). Foucault claims: "And it is the center of the subject's disappearance that philosophical language proceeds as if through a labyrinth, not to recapture him, but to test (and through language itself) the extremity of its loss" (*LCP* 43).

The historical dislocation of the subject-cogito (vis-à-vis Freud) has seen a shift from any placing of "self" in "world" to a semantic (à la structuralism) placing of "Self" in text, and, later, in the postmodern telematic reproduction of images. The influence of structuralism allows us to begin to see a shift in philosophy toward the precedence of language, or a structural-linguistic a priori of human experience. Structuralism holds that the nature of human experience is not in the act of *parole*, the individual utterance, but in the system of language (*langue*) that enables speech and meaning. Now, subjective reality is controlled by the mere substitution of sign-images (advertising). One response to structuralism is evidenced in phenomenology's efforts to reduce the individual's intuitive surface experience to a philosophical structure at a depth that characterizes a more universal, for example, iconistic, experience of contextuality. In its response to Descartes, phenomenology is among the first attempts to construct a scientific method for cutting through appearance to reach an objective (or in the case of Edmund Husserl, "essentialist"), "bracketed" state of consciousness. This occlusion of the subject is the hallmark of structuralism and objective science.

The evolution of this problematic is worked out in the poststructural linguistics of Jacques Derrida, who argues that the relationships between sign and signifier, between writing and conceptual image, between discourse and subject, are not held in stable correspondence. In an arbitrary system of substitutions and differences, the meaning of any signified is perpetually deferred outside itself along a chain of signifiers; thus, the "presence" of meaning is illusory at best. It is easy to see how antihumanist philosophy culminated with deconstruction—wherein the signified "man" escapes, deferring forever away from itself, infinitely (dis)appearing, through the discourse that has propagated the image of "man" for the past two centuries. From the French affirmation of the "decentered subject," to the sovereignty of absence in the linguistic systems of Ferdinand de Saussure and Derrida, as Kroker and David Cook put it, in postmodernism: "everything is coming up signs" (*PS* 77). In the poststructural metaphysical system of grammatology, everything from power to meaning can only be evaluated in terms of absence and emptiness—it is a culture of nihilism.

Foucault warned of the disappearance of "man" (doubling into signs) for the same reasons why Nietzsche proclaimed that there was no God—because we have killed him, along with Nature, in our will to "double" or exchange everything. Nietzsche foresaw "that the postmodernist (and thus nihilistic) imagination always begins with the world in reverse image (the real as the site of exterminism)" (*PS* 33). Here theories are exchanged for Being, science for

God, and dollar signs ($) for human value. Along these lines "man's" emergence as the centered discourse of the nineteenth-century episteme placed it merely in discourse. As language itself reclaims center stage our focus returns to decentered discourse, to the awareness of language as only representation in a technologically saturated, or techno-real, culture. When the distinction between reality and appearance collapse, leaving only hyperreality and simulacra, humanity finds itself in the presence of a collapsing sign/power system. Foucault suggests: "Man is in the process of perishing as the being of language continues to shine ever brighter upon our horizon" (*OT* 386).

Where should one look for ethical-political discourse that addresses the postmodern problematic of the disembodied individual—"man"? Jurgen Habermas places much theoretical attention on communicational and normative language concerns in relation to Otherness in the postmodern culture, and deservedly so. But while our attention has been on the Other, the individual has gradually been rescripted into (and superimposed onto) the technology of the age, a movement Habermas would valorize as a dissolution of "self" into contradictory codes and relations (Lyotard xviii). Though the potential answers to this question may now seem equivocal and indefinite, there is a sense of movement toward a horizon of postpostmodernity from which something affirmative must emerge. Richard Rorty's pragmatism is a tribute to the concern of philosophy with this matter. But Rorty's work, though diligent, stays within institutional and traditional polemical boundaries. Bauldrillard and Lyotard challenge the ethical import of the technological narrative on humanistic grounds with a more compelling account of postmodernity. Of course, the attempt to establish a clear-cut ethical agenda for each of these theorists would prove to be fruitless. The point here is not merely to establish a philosophical framework by which to examine the complex material and institutional dimensions of legitimation for the discourses that consume the individual, but to evaluate at this important historical juncture the fissures and folds that open up new spaces for experience. This is precisely the opportunity that these writings present us with in *Reading Simulacra*.

At this historical impasse in the representational account of knowledge, a pragmatic line is most likely to be adopted. John Dewey and Foucault alike would find encouragement in the liberation from the notion of "man" as "transcendental or enduring subject" because it, as such a subject, is something society can repress. (*CP* 206-207). Nietzsche speaks of overcoming "the self" and its subjugation to the social will. In this light, Giles Deleuze and Felix Guattari hold:

> The human and social sciences have accustomed us to see the figure of Man behind every social event... Such forms of knowledge project an image of reality at the expense of reality itself. They talk figures and icons and signs, but fail to perceive forces and flows. They blind us to other realities, and especially the reality of power as it subjugates us. Their function is to tame, and the result is the fabrication of docile and obedient subjects. (*AO* xx)

Following Nietzsche, Foucault declares that "man" will disappear again as soon as knowledge discovers a new form (*OT* 386-387). For Foucault, the subject is always subjugated to the configurations of power and knowledge, whether disciplinary, institutional, or discursive. But it may soon escape the will to power of classical thought only to realize more contemporary social and technological forces entrapping the individual within the power/knowledge grid.

Today, the screen replaces the social sciences as the instrument of social domination by which operative mechanics are now inscribed on the individual. "Man" becomes the object of statistical study in market surveys and political polls—his destiny is that of the technological model (or the DNA code). Prediction and control of the body are the domain of technology. Postmodern humans are, quite literally, experiencing the "bodily invasion" of "a seemingly endless flow of inFORMational bits and pieces, fragments of a world that never existed, electronic [fascinations] that have no substance independent of the simulative re-structuring of experience" (Pfohl 7). Everywhere around us, "hot" lived experiences are being replaced by "cool"[1] technological media (the television set stands in for the trip to the zoo or the ballpark; in vitro fertilization substitutes for real sex; computers replace thought). At this point of digital bliss, TV replaces, or at least mediates, real life to such an extent that it ontologically pluralizes (TV-Being) the realm of possibilities for lived experiences. Many of us are like "Thanatoids" in Thomas Pynchon's *Vineland*, stuck in limbo between life (real lived experiences that are being evacuated for simulations everywhere around us) and death (TV mediated experiences, or simulacra) (McHale 139-141). For Arthur Kroker, the major philosophical question today becomes: "TV or not TV?" In incessant TV-flow: "everything which escapes the real world of TV, everything which is not videated as its identity-principle, everything which is not processed through TV . . . is peripheral" (*PS* 268). Is TV-Being redeemable?

In this (cathode) light, Dewey and Foucault would surely agree with the need to get beyond traditional notions of subjectivity, objectivity, and truth (*CP* 204) in order to emancipate the individual from these operational/technological forms of death. The question remains: is it possible to embrace this account of "man" as the shape of power relations being meshed out, today formed in the interrelations of the technocratic discourses and produced on the screen, and then turn to a pragmatic concern for a better set of social constructs, whereby such notions such as "truth," "culture," "freedom," "power," and "knowledge," are relevant only as they "facilitate the creation of a new and better sort of human being" (*RP* 10)? In other words, is it possible to "will," in a Nietzschean spirit, beyond these fatal strategies in life-affirming ways (Baudrillard's apprehension, Kroker's invitation)? Or is humanity moving ever faster to the cyber-call of William Gibson's *Neuromancer*, toward a state of symbiosis with the machine, which issues in the end of lived experiences for human beings and the entry into a simulated, virtual or cybernetic world of existence?

In 1926 Dewey's concern with establishing a socially relevant philosophy was a response to the developing crises of legitimation in metaphysical and epistemological discourses, now fully realized in what can be called the "postscientific age." An increasing incredulity toward traditional "representational" philosophical metanarratives, corollary with the development of a polyvocal science narrative, has turned into acute sensitivity during the present era of postmodernity—a sensitivity that has brought contemporary philosophy to a crucial concern for the "individual." Foucault posits that social mechanisms of control spread out in a system of relations typically accorded a scientific status. Such a master-narrative interpenetrated by science, technology, knowledge relations, and other discourses of "normalization invade our language and our institutions" (White 18). Philosophers such as Lyotard and Baudrillard see knowledge-claims in the postmodern society as a functioning pragmatics of language games, in which technological proliferation is the legitimizing operative (Lyotard xxv). Baudrillard is often concerned with communication and the technological circulation of images and signs where "the image has become less the expression of an individual subject than the commodity of an anonymous consumerist technology" (Zerzan 19). On the other hand, Lyotard focuses on the technological transformation of information into the language of computers, stripping it of use-value that translates into a mercantilization and exploitation of knowledge itself. Such an ideology of communicational transparency and concern for the commoditization of knowledge goes hand in hand with the philosopher's attention to socio-ethical concerns since philosophy sees its own ethical and political discourses legitimatized in its interlinkage with the heretofore centered scientific discourse. Since Nietzsche, it is not philosophy, but the field of positive sciences in which truths and essentials have been determined for the past century. Now that technology is akin to knowledge, validity and truth have been replaced by efficiency and performability. Technology is allied with contemporary knowledge through the efficiency by which it "reinforces" reality (Lyotard 46). In other words, good performance allows more effective verification, and simultaneously increases the ability to be "right." In this sense, technological performance is a self-legitimizing system of power taking the form of data accessibility, data processing, and information control. But where is humanity located within this new technological paradigm?

For Lyotard, the desperate methods of scientific legitimation are events of language games between language users. The communication of utterances is a situational as well as a performative "gesture." The maneuvers of this newly technological game are governed by rules; for example, the sender is placed in a role of control and expects the receiver to perform according to contextually prescribed conventions, some explicit, some not. What is important here is not so much Lyotard's working out of the dynamics of language games, which he shows to replace traditional narrative knowledge with a more localized digital one, but recognizing their inextricable social penetration. Performativity occurs along sociolinguistic relations that include the domain of the subject. The game has channeled into the circuitry of technology; the arena is society, and the individual, or subject, moves, is positioned, placed in response to the technocratic discourse. As Lyotard notes, the "organic self exists in a fabric of relations more complex and mobile than ever before" (15). One is always located at "nodal points" (15) of communication circuits, posts through which information passes. The transparency of the sign so easily encodes the subject that it has become fractal, tending to disappear into the representational networks of technological commentary and computerized control—the ubiquitous flow of signs, messages, and consumer codes that compose the "white noise" engulfing us.

In the work of Baudrillard, one encounters a modern subjectivity in which the industrialization of language has culminated in the circulation and reproduction (signing) of the image of "man." The image of the postmodern individual is extremely sophisticated, a high-tech, state-of-the-art reprocessing and instantaneous transmission that condenses the conceptual differences of time and space. It is a screenal image, one in which the subject, has become the electronic object. Alice Jardine writes that the historical development of photography turned "man" into an object, or "froze" him and "'a space consciously elaborated by Man is replaced by one where he operates consciously.' A new space, which was suddenly larger (or smaller) than Man, found a language, began to objectify Man, to turn him into an image" (74). Today, the mirror or photographic image no longer "represents" the subject—all that implodes in simulation. The systems of simulation and screenal image processing are the subject's new locutionary territories. Douglas Kellner asserts: "The subject, then, becomes transformed into an object as part of a nexus of information and communication networks" (71). That process serves to "turn the individual into a new cultural object; an object who produces cultural knowledge and cultural texts via the new informational formats" (Denzin 8). Quite literally, the postmodern individual is possessed by the "screen" of TV, video, and computers that capture its image. Everyday events become media dramas, and lifestyles become coded representations of reality controlled by video processing (12). Baudrillard observes that today "the scene and the mirror have given way to a screen and a network. There is no longer any transcendence or depth, but only the immanent surface of operations unfolding, the smooth and functional surface of communication . . . the surrounding universe and our very bodies are becoming monitoring screens" (*EC* 12). Our displaced bodies have become objects of continuity and feedback with the screen—a general interface that drives toward "homogenization in a single virtual process" (*FS* 66), one dominated by the logic of late-capitalist consumer culture and manufactured by the simulation industry, where, as AT&T says: "There is only here."

The electronic Dasein is at once here and not here, here and there, within the space of the screen, within the space of a studio, within the space of a cable, and in transmission to a satellite in space. And now, the microconstruction of the body has entered the totalitarian realm of sensory image. Tiny links in milliseconds instantaneously and continuously flash on the screen to create a procession of images. The macro-experience is evidenced by the advertising industry's method of hypertextually flashing body-images on the screen. Kroker writes: "Everywhere today the aestheticization of the body and its dissolution into a semiurgy of floating body parts reveals that we are being processed through a media scene consisting of our own (externalized) body organs in the form of second order simulacra" (*BI* 21). This telematic model locates the ecstatic "body" within the space of the screen—which is itself nothing more than a site for information processing and communication. This site of "doubling" is the controlling space of computer data banks (on each individual including age, health, marital status, and financial status), lifestyle marketing, and wide-screen TVs—the microphysics of an anonymous power that one invests by consuming it. It is just like in George Orwell's *1984*, only now it is not Big Brother watching us, but us voluntarily watching and submitting to it: "Oh, look, I'm on video!" she exclaims while unwittingly under the enchantment of the surveillance loop (i.e., we monitor ourselves by conforming to what is seen on TV).

The transformation of "discursive" into "technological" colonization of "the human" is easily explainable. As Foucault said: "The body is the inscribed surface of events (traced by language and dissolved by ideas), the locus of a dissociated Self" (*LCP* 148). In the development of the social and physical sciences, the body (as an "inscribed surface of events"—economic, political, HIStorical, biological) and the signifier "man" (as traced in language) have been overcoded and transmuted through a proliferation of discourse now located in the power/knowledge folds of a cybernetic universe (e.g., advertising and media representations). Today: "[i]n postmodern society, linguistic rituals of representation are being rapidly transformed into cybernetically codified rites of 'signing'" (Pfohl 8). In this "ultramodern conjunction of power and knowledge" (5), the technocratic culture legitimizes this dimension of a new masternarrative (tele-electronic "will to power") in which humanity serves as the host of this parasitic space. Through complex networks of interactive living (everything from teleconferences to video classrooms, to virtual bulletin boards, to the home shopping network), human subjectivity is lured into a decentered cyberspace. Stephen Pfohl remarks:

> Drawn into the dense, high speed and electronically pulsating structural operations of telecommunicative mass marketing, many of our bodies are literally invaded and then extended outward into the networking of the media itself. Multiple channels of inFORMation converge on and through us . . . Perhaps this is because those of us most subject to the cybernetic codings of ultramodern power are finding ourselves situated physically within such a serial swell of data that even our most intimate senses of what's real become extended outward into ever more enveloping inFORMational

networks. At the same time, the sensational effects of these network hookups feed back upon our supposedly "inner selves," reconstituting a great many of our lived sensory imaginations of what's (empirically) possible and what's (k)not. (18)

No longer able to distinguish outside from an inside, Self from Other, real from image, sign from referent, everything implodes at the subject's "eye/I" (59). The TV screen or computer monitor is the new locus of the individual. In this sense, "man" has become the focus of interlocution—outside the screen lies our experience of the data, the image projected on the object; inside the screen "man" is the image itself. In this astral and translucent site, the immanent reversibility between subject and object is evident.

The electronic "materiality" of "man" has created the perfect Object of simulation. For Critical Art Ensemble, the electronic body is the last frontier of real signification and perfect representation. Without absence on the screen, it appears as pure presence. It holds absolute meaning, devoid of referentials. Having escaped the economy of desire, it is "free of becoming" (*ED* 73). Baudrillard observes this metamorphosis in which "Meaning does not slip from one form to the other, it is the forms which slip directly from one to the other, as in dance movements or in oracular prophecies . . . [as] a body freed from all subjectivity, a body recovering the animal felinity of the pure object, of pure movement, of a pure gestural transpiration" (*EC* 46). The desire of the subject to be free, to be autonomous, is fatally seduced by a passion for the Object. Now simulation is the object of our desire. The seduction of simulation is pure desire. It translates into a colonization of the real through a kind of self-legitimation where performativity of simulation becomes the operative mechanics. The televisual Object serves as the locus of this seduction; it exists only as a pure model of simulation, artificially reproduced. This seduction is dangerous to the subject: the "object has become the subject's mode of disappearance" (*EC* 97). Since the "[o]bject is without finitude and without desire, for it has already reached its end—it stays perpetually enigmatic for the subject. . . . The object is therefore inaccessible to the subject's knowledge, since there can be no knowledge of that which already has complete meaning" (*EC* 89). The screenal body is the object of desire (private telematics): it is there, in its entirety—surface is depth. Its circulation is the order of the disappearance of the subject. As Baudrillard insists: "It is this promiscuity and the ubiquity of images, this viral contamination of things by images, which are the fatal characteristics of our culture" (*EC* 35).

What is left outside the screen? As the electronic sign becomes a referent to the flesh, the reality, the humanity, and the complexity of the body with organs and tissues, is abandoned. Void of depth, the body becomes a "Xerox" of itself: "It is paper onto which designer gender, ethnicity, and lifestyle are inscribed" (*ED* 73). The only "body" that is of value to the world is the networks, the terminals, and the capacitors that circulate, store, and enhance the image—the desired commodity of the techno-real culture. Ecstasy comes now from the object, from watching it, repetitiously; it is obscene (more visible than visible). People are seduced by the power to electronically displace the body, to miniaturize the gestures into automatic time and space, preserved in "infinitesimal memory and the screen" (Baudrillard 17). This includes the computer screen and the telemonitor—the screenal file of information pulled up by the request for "'social security number," the place of pure representation (data is without flaw) of the new technological individual. Baudrillard adds: "The time has come of a miniaturization of time, bodies, pleasures. There is no longer any ideal principle for these things on the scale of the human . . . . this body, our body, appears basically superfluous, useless in the extension, multiplicity and complexity of its organs, tissues, functions" (*FS* 66).

The "real" body now can only objectify itself in the appearance of the commodity. According to Fredric Jameson, in his introduction to Lyotard's "Report," the sense of obscenity raised by the increasing mechanization of circulation is symptomatic of the commodity fetishism of late-capitalism. The commodity fetish, writes L. Jonathan Beller "marks the desire to convert exchange value into use value, to free the object from the tyranny of circulation, and to possess it" (para. 24 *Postmodern Culture*). The screen is the remaining sphere for colonization of the commodity (as information bits and entertainment). Jameson refers to Guy Debord in saying that the circulation of image is "the last stage of commodity reification" (Lyotard xv). When the commodity becomes nonphysical, all that remains is the pure mode of production—the acceleration of efficiency and performance. The electronic medium now produces the organic body as a commodified space for signification. "The commodity-body is reduced to a pure equivalence" with its image, where "becoming" translates into having (Massumi 129). Celeste Olaquiaga asserts: "The last bastion of a precarious sense of identity, the body has turned into the ruin of its own image: against senility, disability, and physical decay, mass culture projects images of immaculate health and happiness, and ultimately the cybernetic, or half technological body" (11).

In this gesture, the individual has become the locus for the circulation and production of paranoic signs (of economy, desire, and the body). Consumption of signification is our pure function; it is the only way to make us appear more like the electronic body. Individuals are desiring machines—bodies without organs, transformed into living screens that serve as sites for the circulation of advertising codes. Access to the signs of beauty, health, wealth, and happiness are all there for us. There is no depth; all meaning is superficial; just look at any jeans ad in which signifiers for sex are everywhere; but what about the signifieds? Or the ambivalence of Nike's "Just do it" ads: Just do what? Just supply the signified, ultimately in some form of consumption (the transcendental signifier is no longer the phallus, but the sign of consumption—"$").

The technological overcoding and hypersignification of the sign colonizes the individual's identity, body, and psyche through a powerful new semiurgy—a fatal state of a perpetual simulacrum in which the consumer-subject finds it(self) ritually processing signs. For some time now, one can only see the enterprise of late-capitalism as the exploitation of the individual. As Pfohl puts it: "[W]hat may seem like the 'unmediated' experience of 'empowering affect' may in reality be little but the nearly instantaneous 'possession' of our bodies by an ultramodern mechanics of inFORMmation. For want of better words, this is a way of describing the whitemale driven and cybernetic culture of contemporary CAPITAL" (256). Deleuze and Guattari warn us in *Anti-Oedipus* that the schizophrenic ethic they propose is simply a way of surviving under capitalism—a way of finding new avenues for desires within the capitalist mode of production that otherwise ritually dissolves human experience into a network of electronic effects.

Can contemporary theory provide an alternative narrative to the telematic model of power relations that overcode the body? The Deleuzian model suggests that it may be possible for the postmodern subject, as a continual body without organs (BwO), to resist these new sociological and technological systems of control: advertising, electronic surveillance, social security numbers, AIDS records, and so forth. Nomadic desire is the power of "becoming" across deterritorialized social technologies—cyperspace as the electronic BwO. The circulation and overproduction of "man"—the screenal image constitutes Critical Art Ensemble's (CAE) theoretical (mis)reading of the BwO and initiates the transformation or deterritorialization of the Body Without Organs of Deleuze and Guattari into the "electronic body" of CAE. Referring to the televisual body, they write: "The electronic body looks so real. It moves around, it gazes back, it communicates. Its appearance is our appearance. Identity manifests and is reinforced, as subjectivity is extracted/imposed by the electronic other" (*ED* 70). The BwO is "more real" than the corporeal body, because it can be maintained and contained within the delineation that silhouettes it on the screen. Free of the flesh, there is no need for deodorant, shampoo or Grecian Formula—it is a static body, indefinite and without need for change. The seduction of telematics lies in the isolation of desire—a perfect body sovereign in absolute space of simulation, and existing without absence: "The electronic body seduces those who see it into the bliss of counter-production by offering the hope of bodily unity that transcends consumption. But the poor, pathetic, organic body is always in a state of becoming. If it consumed just one more product, perhaps it might become whole, perhaps it too could become a body without organs existing in electronic space" (*ED* 77). The electronic body as a perfect body without organs feels no pain as it oscillates on the screen. Thus: "we must eternally consume something to make our appearance more like its appearance" (*ED* 70-71).

Intermedia artwork and telecritical performances such as "BwO Now" [2] by Critical Art Ensemble calls attention to the electronic bunkers of recombinant culture that colonize both the public and private sphere via a screenal landscaping of desire: "[t]he economy of desire can be safely viewed through the familiar window of screenal space. Secure in the electronic bunker, a life of alienated auto-experience (a loss of the social) can continue in quiet acquiescence and deep privation. The viewer is brought to the world, the world to the viewer, all mediated through the ideology of the screen. This is virtual life in a virtual world" (*ED* 28). Why desire anything—everything is already programmed for you and only awaits its return in the "on" switch of the remote control. Many of us are vulnerable to finding our(selves)—our lived perceptions of our identities and our potential as human beings—channeled through the feedback from the television, the video loop of preprocessed images. Pfhol writes of this occurrence:

> Too many of us today are ritually inFORMed about who we are, what we fear and desire, and what we might purchase through a dense and high speed circulation of electronically-mediated images. And so we are lured into the aestheticized fascinations of fascism. Screen to screen, advert to advert . . . the pornographic quality of becoming almost fully commodified. A living doll. The word made advert then flesh. The ideal model. The simulacrum. (36)

On a *48 Hours* episode about the American fascination with televisual fame, Tom Brokaw reminds us that, contrary to popular belief (e.g., Warhol's "fifteen minutes" à la Darva Conger), it is still possible to live valuable "real" lives without being on TV. Collective strategies of resistance to the ideology of the screen include exacerbating those moments of incarnation when the BwO might appear as flesh in decay (i.e, in the celebrity). For example, O. J. Simpson's anguishing face, or the vomiting President Bush in China. During these times of possession, the BwO is "most vulnerable to organic deficiencies" (*ED* 75). Accordingly, passive addiction and hyperconsumption must be avoided. Decentralized programming, noncommercialized television (all news and sporting events, and even so-called public access programs, are brought to us by a sponsor), and free access to the airwaves could return some sovereignty to the individual (*ED* 135).

Baudrillard posits a contemporary strategy of "seduction" that concerns the disappearance of the individual into "ever more sophisticated methods of biological and molecular control and retrieval of bodies" (*EC* 74). Our response may only be to embrace the destiny of simulation—which is the same as "man's" own destiny, to disappear: "And the destiny of signs," he continues, "is to be torn from their destination, deviated, displaced, diverted, recuperated, seduced" (*EC* 80). According to Baudrillard "the entire strategy of seduction is to bring things to a state of pure appearance, to make them radiate and wear themselves out in the game of appearances . . . only the visible has any value for us. . . . Everywhere one seeks to produce meaning, to make the world signify, to render it visible. We are not, however, in danger of lacking meaning; quite to the contrary, we are gorged with meaning and it is killing us" (*EC* 63). Pure appearance is the fatal characteristic of simulation—the same fatality of social systems, of knowledge/power relations, of historical epochs. Bauldrillard asserts: "The present system of dissuasion and simulation succeeds in neutralizing all finalities, all referential, all meanings" (*EC* 74). Simulation that becomes pure appearance invites an implosion of meaning. Nietzsche warned us against such "neutrality" in the days of the (electronic ?) "will to will."

In a purely perspectival existence the proximity of the object and the instantaneity of all meaning invites the "schizophrenic" ethics of Deleuze and Guattari. Such an ethics may allow technology to be celebrated for its socially pluralizing potential. This is why performances by collectives such as Critical Art Ensemble,[3] and postmodern writing by authors such as Reese Williams and Kathy Acker, have become art forms of vast sociological import. The transgressive language and images within their texts overcode and hypersignify history, technology, and the postmodern colonization of the subject (desire), pushing them to ultimate levels of signification, and in the process descripting the material coding system of our late-capitalist consumer culture. However, Pfohl pronounces his reservations concerning the rhizomatic drifts and ruptures in "ultramodern power" that this sort of reading offers:

> Unfortunately, material access to spaces in excess of the dominant order is exactly what is being denied us in the emergence of ultramodern society. The more we move within the dense and high speed world of image simulations that characterize the ultramodern, the more we find excess modeled to fit prepackaged formats of access and then sold back to us so that we might consume what's different and what's the same in the same bite/byte. (16)

Returning again to Nietzsche, in the closed technological circuitry of the media and television, where experiences are virtually recycled, things appear meaningful only if familiar within existing (his)torical structures when appearing as premodeled images, and differences become "real" only when represented, doubled, or otherwise simulated (22).

For Baudrillard and for other postmodern theorists, there is no escaping the destiny of the object nor the seduction of the transparency of the fully functional sign. But the legitimacy of the scientific narrative itself is brought into question when representation is seen for what it is—"a reproduction, for subjectivity, of an objectivity that lies outside of it—[that] projects a mirror theory of knowledge and art, whose fundamental evaluative categories are those of adequacy, accuracy, and Truth" (Lyotard viii). The breakdown of these "foundationalist" categories (as Rorty would have it) symptomitizes the crises of representation, and recasts a postreferential epistemology. In this fissure within the central current of the grand narrative of representation, "man" dissolves (Foucault 386), seized by the vertigo of reproduction and simulation.

Yet, here, technology can be celebrated for bringing us to the brink of a caesura by which the conditions of Foucault's first epoch are recoverable—that period when objects were saturated with signification—and a new, different space for "humanity" may yet open. Hence, the postmodern scene.

Chapter Two

Nietzsche's Legacy: The Postmodern Will

> This world is the will to power—and nothing besides! And you are the will to power and nothing besides!
>
> —Nietzsche, *The Will to Power*

Friedrich Nietzsche's profound influence on (post)modernity has been far-reaching and stems back to prophetic observations he made as a late nineteenth-century writer. Nietzsche recognized the influence that Rationalism, and its claims of Truth, would have on the impending modern age. Like the madman who proclaims "God is Dead" in *The Gay Science*, Nietzsche himself could only heretically forecast the revolutionary impact that the "panacea" of science, and later technology, would have on the order of things. Along with God, Man, and Nature, Truth would lose its place as absolute.

Nietzsche's critique of rationalist eschatology did not end here. Written following the creative and celebratory masterpiece of the (metaphoric) Overman and "the will" *(Thus Spoke Zarathustra)*, *Beyond Good and Evil* begins with a rebuke of the energies of philosophers. Nietzsche considered the philosophical essentialism of the "will to truth" as the "hazardous" metaphysical tyranny through which humanity would derive, from the transitory and seductive world, immutable and perfect. Western metaphysicians have used such notions of "truths" and "essences" to convince us that their ideal world is somehow more real than the "deceptive" and changing (real) one of "becoming" (33-34). It is in *Beyond Good and Evil* that Nietzsche explains for us in terse prose what he had described in narrative metaphor in *Thus Spoke Zarathustra*—the deadly processes of reversal of existence in a changing corporeal world for the fictitious and unattainable "thing-in-itself." These matters were foretold by Nietzsche as "the advent of nihilism" (*WP* 3). The nihilistic will imposes upon "becoming" the character of *being* (*Zarathustra 113*) and devalues the world in a drive "to pass sentence on this whole world of becoming as a deception and to invent a world beyond it, a *true world*" (*WP* 13). It was "Nietzsche's accusations that in a world in which conditions of existence are transposed into 'predicates of being,' it would be the human fate to live through a fantastic inversion and cancellation of the order of the real" (*PS* 31). From this reversal of realities for "truths," what is left are only (distorted) constructs of existence. These constructs are merely illusions created by humanity that serve to fulfill its need for stability and simplification. Our metaphysical systems have tended to associate Truth with depths—the essence behind appearance—and with uncovering the elements of Being. This fatal process "falsely project[s] into the essence of things" (*WP* 14) a state of "being" by which all reality is judged as merely "apparent."

To Nietzsche, the "apparent world" of reality is a world of "perspectival appearances," or "wills" (*WP* 15). Through the will humanity imposes "truth" on things. In this scenario, truth always operates as metaphor, anthropomorphism, or (subjective) simulation. At the heart of the will is the nihilistic characteristic of rationalist thought (subject/object split) which ritually doubles nature/reality and fills the lack with language. In subverting the Classical divisions between what are objective and subjective experiences, interpretive experience enters into the "ritual folds" of language. In this sense, language is not "expressive of some pre-given relation between a (potentially) all knowing subject and a fully knowable object, but language [is seen] as a ritual practice that materially gives (and takes away) particular objects to and from (historically specific) subjects" in a ritual of doubles, images, and signs, in short—meaning (Pfohl 83). This exchange ritual involves a sociohistorically and politically conditioned linguistic medium through which fluctuating relations between matter and meaning are reduced to an orderly coexistence for the subject. In other words, Nietzsche's dance of continual *becoming* is fixed in language.

So it follows that the only world that is known to humanity is the world that it can describe in language to itself as subject of language. Jacques Lacan theorizes that at the mirror stage, the infant sees its double and begins to acquire language by which to fill the lack that arises between self and image. With this desire comes symbolic linguistic forms through which the "self" enters into an eternally sliding substitution of signs for the material world surrounding it. This experience is that of human subjectivity. Hence, all subjective reality (which is the only type of "reality" to Nietzsche) is the doubling effect of the language. What is lost in the "doubling effect" of the sign, however, is precisely "the real" itself. Moreover, since all language is arbitrarily constructed meaning that describes the "outside" reality of the "subjective self," there is no Truth, only "perspectival truth effects." The "truth" of language is *inside* of language and nowhere else.[1] Experience loses its "truth" when it is put into language, by making equal things that are not equivalent: a "linguistic reality" makes the referent and the sign seem interchangeable; but this is always falsity. Nietzsche clearly foresaw the fatal effects of Enlightenment thinking and the search for Truth (positivism in sciences and representation in aesthetics) founded in a logocentric ground of human experience. As Mike Gane puts it: "The world becomes a transparent determinant of the sign, is a 'long sermon' [Derrida's phrase] caught within the confines of Western metaphysics" (92). Derrida follows this Nietzschean course in "White Mythologies" with his critique of logocentrism and metaphor (absence) as essential to a metaphysics of representation. Other postphilosophers such as Richard Rorty reverberate similar sentiments of disenchantment with foundational philosophical thought, discarding it for a pragmatist ethics in which truth claims are valid only as contextual belief systems.

The thrust of Western thought has been the delusive drive to replace a real world with the false one called "truth," leaving nothing but a precarious and illusory state of appearances. Because the world is measured in "categories that refer to a purely fictitious world" (*WP* 13), one of the will, there is simply no "true" world whatsoever (*WP* 14). This leaves us with the residual truth that the world is always already an illusory projection. The genealogical undoing of "truth" as an effect of multiple perspectival illusions ends in the postmodern view that "everything is appearance" (Norris 172). Thus, Jean Baudrillard attacks all metaphysical "truths" associated with the realm of depth. Instead of discussing a "truth" behind appearances, he speaks of a "truth *of* appearances" (Singer 140). For example, consider Baudrillard's reading of America as a great free-floating referential fiction.

For Baudrillard, the postmodern condition is the knowledge that "appearance" or the image have passed through the following successive phases: "(1) It is the reflection of a basic reality. (2) It masks and perverts a basic reality. (3) It masks the *absence* of a basic reality. (4) It bears no relation to any reality whatever: it is its own pure simulacrum" (*SIM* 11). The epistemological movement presented here is from the metaphysical idealism of Plato to Nietzschean skepticism and into postmodern cynicism. Postmodernism perceives surface without depth, signs without referents (referring only to other signs), appearances without reality. We have reached the stage where appearances become reality, in which the real is replaced by images that serve as "the real." Look at the case of a public television station that for lack of funds, aired the interior of a fish tank for a number of days, and then when regular programming resumed, they were overwhelmed by a majority of viewers who wanted the "fish tank" back. Now there is a pay-per-view channel offering a continuous, hyperreal "fish tank," where the TV image so easily replaces the real thing, without need to change the water, scrub the glass, or replace deceased fish. Christopher Norris comments on this stage of "hyperreality":

> It is no longer possible to maintain the old economy of truth and representation in a world where "reality" is entirely constructed through forms of mass-media feedback, where values are determined by consumer demand (itself brought about by the endless circulation of meanings, images and advertising codes) [beauty, wealth, and prestige], and where nothing could serve as a means of distinguishing true from merely true-seeming.... (166)

In this scenario, reality only returns according to its programming, and the individual need merely decode the message following the same code: "The equivalent of the total neutralization of signifieds by the code is the instantaneous verdict of fashion or of every billboard or TV advertising message" (*SE&D* 62). The individual who buys merely "reactualizes" the model by operating within the consumer code. Even the object is no longer functional, but "tests" the individual along the same code: "Both object and information already result from selection, an edited sequence of camera angles, they have already tested 'reality' and have only asked those questions to which it has responded" (*SE&D* 63).

What Baudrillard realizes and Nietzsche diagnosed is that reality would always be nothing but an effect of thought, the will, the sign, and now the code (*EDOI* 44). To consider the world as purely objective, as something other than illusion, as reconcilable by some determinate means, is totally futile. One must recognize the reality of illusions (*EDOI* 45). Appearance, as much as reality, is always already nothing but simulation. Following the precession of simulacra, one is left with only the orders of representation, of simulated experience. All experience is of a simulacrum—always already once removed, by being processed through language or coded as cultural text. When the "real" no longer exists as that which can be represented (simulacra are level upon level of representation in which there is no longer a "real" produced), the abstract basis of exchange (real for image, presence for absence) dissolves. Society seems to have slipped past the signifying order by which artifice, power, and meaning itself once operated. Even art, the revered form of artifice (of will and self-creation) for Nietzsche, was destined to disappear. Art is no longer distinct from anything else as a site of representation once the rest of the world, itself, becomes nothing but a hyperaestheticized enclave of (re)presentation. Today, everyday life is aestheticized in the flow of signs, images, and simulations (Featherstone 67). Art is dead, having lost its critical distance from reality, which is inseparable from its own image (*SE&D* 75). Think of inner-city murals, industrial art (steel girders serving as an artifact outside a municipal building in Pittsburgh), or even the latest movie: "Gosh, our fishing trip to the Dakotas was just like *A River Runs Through It.*" Without artifice, the space of illusion is lost. With only the aesthetic play of appearances, one is left with the obscenity of the obvious. Baudrillard comments: "Today art no longer creates anything but the magic of its disappearance" (*FS* 10). Take, for example, art forms that draw attention to themselves as art—no longer providing the illusion of itself as artifice. No longer simply existing as "real" artifice, art is now hyperreal, and it seems our entire media (or screenal) culture operates under this logic of the *trompe l'oeil* come alive.

Baudrillard's early work serves as a genealogy of semiological criticism for a contemporary Marxist thought. [2] Moving from a Saussurian paradigm that insists on the linguistic nature of reality, Baudrillard reduces all "economic, social, and political issues to questions of symbolic exchange" (Norris 188). Then working through an analysis of production and consumption of the object from its use value to exchange value, Baudrillard ends up with a resting place in late-capitalist code that equivocates commodities and signs. In "Consumer Society," Baudrillard posits that the logic of consumption is not based on acquiring the use-value of objects, but operates, instead, under the specific "social function of exchange, communication, and distributions of values within a corpus of signs" (*SW* 46). For example, people use Sure deodorant for "fear of social rejection," buy a Lexus car for "acceptance" at the office, or wear Obsession perfume to "feel sexy." In the shift from commodity to signs (the structural play of value), any chance for a precapitalistic symbolic exchange (of goods exchanged in reciprocation) is overthrown by the operation of the capitalist code (Poster 281). Mark Poster explains that code:

> In contemporary society consumer objects bear signs which have meaning as part of a structure. The signifiers associated with the commodities are autonomous from the labor process that produced the commodities materially. Today, commodities no longer function as use values, as things which serve the needs of the rational individual, rather they are part of the social system of the exchange of meanings. The consumption of an object has more semiological than material significance. (281)

In this now ubiquitous system of signs, simulacra, and digitized codes—"a system with no fixed determinations, a world where everything is both equivalent to and indifferent to everything else" (*SW* 5)—the signified and the referent lose out to the operational surfaces of communication, the abstraction of the media, and the force of the consumer code.

Baudrillard outlines three historical orders of simulacra: the counterfeit (renaissance period), production (industrial era), and simulation (presently dominant): "The first-order simulacrum operates on the natural law of value, the second-order simulacrum on the market law of value, and the third-order simulacrum on the structural law of value" (*SE&D* 50). Every order subsumes the next. According to Baudrillard, the second order of meanings arises with the industrial revolution—where signs and objects become products in series with technology as their origins. It is no longer meaningful to distinguish between counterfeit and origin; the new system of meaning operates according to the law of equivalences and nondifference . . . "it is basically one episode in the line of simulacra, that episode of producing infinite series of potentially identical beings (objects-signs) by means of technics" (*SE&D* 55). Today, production gives way to reproduction and the model. In third-order simulacra, products "are conceived according to their very reproducability, their diffraction from a generative core called a 'model' . . . . Only affiliation to the model has any meaning, since nothing proceeds in accordance with its end any more, but issues instead from the model, the 'signifier of reference,' functioning as a foregone, and the only credible, conclusion" (*SE&D* 56). In fact, a liquidation of meaning is ultimately realized in the pure alternation and indifferent play of signs and circulation of image-commodity.[3] Following this loss of reference from use-values to circulating signs, a sense of vertigo develops. Baudrillard asserts: "We are living the end of exchange [instead—circulation]. . . .Where exchange is no longer possible, we find ourselves in a fatal situation, a situation of destiny" (*FS* 47). Now, a new system of semiological social control emerges: "We have reached the point where 'consumption' has grasped the whole of life; where all activities are sequence in the same combinatorial mode; where the schedule of gratification is outlined in advance, one hour at a time; and where the environment is complete, completely climatized, furnished, and culturalized" (*SW* 33). The force of Western thought (Rationalism, Freudianism, and Capitalism) has always been to impose human models on "becoming" (reality) whereby the end is factored in (design) or meaning is delivered in the coding via signs, so everything occurs as prefabricated simulation.

Our fatality is to have everything happen by design in models, codes, and surveys or media feedback (*FS* 187). Through this new consumer coded social order that relies on the "redoubling" effect of the sign's reversal of the real, there is no longer any original appearance, only return, which is always a death (*SIM* 11). Baudrillard makes it clear that the doubling of the sign or image, its replication, puts an end to "designation." In *Symbolic Exchange and Death* (69), he expounds on the example of an Andy Warhol painting of Marilyn Monroe in which the replicas of her face produce both the death of the original (the first doubling) and the end of representation that is enveloped by simulacra (brought about by the second double—does it refer to the original or to the double?). It is easy to follow how this vertigo of doubling (death of the referent) might continue ad infinitum. Yet, everything is destined to redouble in the return. The first double is into signs; the second is occurrence. This has been the course of Western metaphysics and essentialism—the fatal strategies of the "always already"—in which Platonic form which precedes life (sign, double, and image), awaits a return (redoubling in existence), which is its death. With Plato, the ideal form (image) prefigures all the imperfect simulations. Nietzsche derides Enlightenment as well as classical reason. He also voices his pessimism about the philosophical historicism of Hegel: "If every result contains within itself a rational necessity, if every event is the victory . . . of the 'idea'—then quickly kneel and go down the whole 'stepladder' of 'results' upon your knees" (qtd. in Lowith 180). The "fatal strategies" then—of epistemology, social sciences, capitalism, philosophy, and so forth—have propelled us to this crucial stage of meaning, where truth, reality, history, and the body, threaten to disappear into simulacra. This "fatality" is the postmodern ecstasy of finalities—the always already that equates difference with "same." Finality is our destiny, where the event is always already a *trace* in language and its signing is just its occurrence as simulation. Even physiology finds itself among the simulacra with the development of biological mapping of DNA, the random inscription of genetic code: "We are in a transfinite universe" (*FS* 70), one of multi-ordered simulacra where we must "will to will."

But this destiny was nothing new for Nietzsche. Zarathustra continually summoned this "going under" of our contemporary systems of thought, so that those who would hear could "go over." Zarathustra remarks: "I am a rail by the river—grasp me who can" (qtd. in Lowith 193). Nietzsche recognized the antinomies inherent in existence when the "will" is an imperative condition in which creativity in metaphor, language, and sameness, must continually be exchanged for difference and then return again and again. He writes that the "essential feature" of *our* nihilistic thought "is fitting new material [perceptions and experiences] into old schemas . . . making equal what is new" (*WP* 273). The destiny of difference is *always already* prescribed in fatal models, systems, metaphors, or signs. It is always a return of difference to the same in an exchange that brings simulacrum, where the same is represented (through difference) ad infinitum. The eternal return of the same occurs daily on WDFM radio that "keeps the 70s alive" three hundred and sixty-five days a year by replaying it, reduplicating it continuously. But this happens all around us, all the time, in postmodern culture—just like detergent advertisers who cannot deliver on their promise of something new, and Monty Python who teases us before its latest parody "and now for something really different." Or look at television reruns and commercials (both ideologically coded representations of family, marriage, patriarchy, etc.) that return again and again in repetition, as coded event scenes. Difference is destined to return, and the return is its death. This fatal activity is the "going under" that calls to the Overman of Nietzsche. But the Overman recognizes "difference" and masters the will by invoking new interpretations (never stable systems). The Overman rejects Truth for a transitory world of constructive and deconstructive forces in eternal return through which a greater "self" may be sculpted or artistically created (*WP* 539).

Nietzsche foresaw a world of wills in which the "will" is masked in myth, morality, philosophy, law, and systems that would overcome those with weaker wills. Here the "will to power" is one of battling perspectives. As Arthur Kroker explains: "Power as 'perspectival appearances' [is] an inverted order of reality with the power of death over life; the reign of 'apparent unities'; the 'fictions' of form, species, law, ego, morality, and purpose" (*PS* 127–128). Nietzsche summons the Overman, who escapes these traps of humanism and metaphysics ("overcomes" himself as human). His "dance" is an "active forgetting" of questions of Being and systems of Truth. Just "become"—in Dionysian laughter. He practices the joy of forgetting in a world free of "truths" and origin, a world of active interpretation—the affirmation of a transitory world. Every individual will is left to create its own perspectival world according to its "measure of unbelief" (*WP* 14). As Nietzsche asserted, the "will to power" lies in the denial of a truthful world: "It is the measure of strength to what extent we can admit to ourselves, without perishing, the merely apparent character, the necessity of lies" (*WP* 15). At the end of *The Will To Power*, Nietzsche confirms: "no longer the humble expression, "'everything is *merely* subjective,'" but "'it is also *our* work!—Let us be proud of it!'"(545).

In Nietzsche's writing, one discovers that the nihilistic "will" that denies a "truthful world" is nothing less than the necessary locus where human experience exchanges reality for illusion, experience for artifice, and the world for metaphor. The will to power, then, always operates by substituting representation for reality, being for becoming, dominion for freedom. Reality, as a perspectival effect of the sign, exists in the circular motion by which "being" is exchanged for "becoming," the double movement of creation and cancellation (*PS* 99). This sacrificial cancellation, or signing, of life by death (redoubling) takes many shapes. Art is the extreme creative "will to power" that gives form to chaos in a mixture of Dionysian and Apollonian impulses, the warring properties of human existence. The figurative drive, the impulse to metaphor, is the "will to power." To will to power is to create, to annihilate, and to will again. Nietzsche acknowledges: "An antimetaphysical view of the world—yes, but an artistic one" (WP 539). In *Twilight of the Idols*, Nietzsche adds: "That the artist places a higher value on appearance than on reality constitutes no objection to the proposition [nihilism]. For 'appearance' here signifies reality *once more*, only selected, strengthened, corrected. . . . The tragic artist is *not* a pessimist—it is precisely he who *affirms* all that is questionable and terrible in existence, he is Dionysian" (39). Zarathustra warned us about the necessity of maintaining the infinite *Dionysian* drift of the sign versus the Apollonian form. The Apollonian turns the slippage and alterity of the Dionysian into a simulacrum. We must balance "difference" in the living language and mother tongue against the "dead" language of simulacrum (*EOO* 21).

The postmodern age reveals the meeting of nihilism and the sign, where experience is structured according to Nietzsche's "will to will." The will, as perspectival space itself, exists only as a lack, or void, and operates as a multiplicity of "truth effects" (*PS* 99). Kroker declares: "Having no (real) existence of its own, the will discovers its truth-value (Nietzsche's 'fictions') in a dominion of signs which undergo an endless metamorphosis in a mirrored world of tautology, metaphor, and simulation" (*PS* 126). As the perspectival space of simulation, the will operates by emptying out the real and reducing experience to a semiological system of abstraction and equivocation of differences (*PS* 130). In simulacra, life is sacrificed to death, real to image, and world to metaphor. For in the postmodern will, experience announces itself as simulacra—the vortex of simulated nothingness (*PS* 118). Kroker writes:

> Baudrillard's notion of the will (and thus power) as a "simulation" of the real signifies that a dramatic reversal of the void/being has occurred. At the "center" of the dead will, there exists in seductive, but paradoxical, form a "plenitude of the void"; and only outside the seduction of the void does there exist that now real lack: the *emptiness* of being. The will as only a "space of simulation" works its optical effect through a reversal of nothingness: it is not so much that "nothingness is not" as that "nothingness *is* being." (*PS* 100)

To enter this vortex is the challenge to the Overman. To will to power is to affirm life in the face of nihilism, to surmount our "Being" human. But in this motion of the postmodern will resides the entire liquidation of the "real" (the void filled by illusion) into the hyperreal (representations thereof). In the genealogy of the hyperreal, the "real space" between the sign and its referent (that of apparent truth) empties into simulacra. The evolution of simulacra means that even the illusion of artifice for Nietzsche now also disappears and becomes just another set of signs.

The processes and tendencies of philosophy, the will to truth and knowledge, the drive toward objectivity, all propagate the loss of illusion. In a very Nietzschean manner, these strategies drive to nihilism—a "going under," since things are meaningless unless transfigured by illusion. Humanity has entered into the scandalous antinomy—to pass over entails the erasure of the subject, and possibly all things human: "The limit of disillusion is that of death," writes Baudrillard (*FS* 51). In Baudrillard's work, our nihilistic will to represent the real—the will to double, to return—the futile process by which life is made "meaningful," is now recognized as "in vain." These fatal strategies erase differences, replace "becoming" with "sameness," and lead into proliferating simulacra. Our fascination with overcoming occurrence by design has only brought us to face the void and the simulacra that fill it. Baudrillard argues: "When knowledge, through models, anticipates the event, in other words, when the event (or opinion) is preceded by its degraded form (or its simulated form) its energy is entirely absorbed into the void" (*FS* 91). Here, Baudrillard's philosophy moves toward death (death of the social, death of difference, death of meaning, or death of the future as an eternally reconstituted past). As one possibility of existence, Baudrillard offers what he calls the "orbital or perspectival possibility," a "simulated generation of differences" (*SIM* 4). This is an attempt to salvage theory and its objects (humanity, culture, and the sign) in the present order of simulation, although, as Norris criticizes: "It is a vision that should bring great comfort to PR experts, campaign managers, media watch-dogs, Pentagon spokesmen and others with an interest in maintaining this state of affairs" (190). Postmodernism is neither pessimistic nor optimistic; it is simply posthistorical, postmeaning and hypereverything—a matter of "survival among the remnants" (*BL* 95). This is the fate we are currently living—the destiny of the will for Nietzsche's "last man."

Baudrillard's analysis operates under the thesis that the world has entered this phase of catastrophic cultural implosion. His conception of the postmodern world is no longer one of dialectical struggle, but one sustained by the logic of a redoubling spiral—the object in its pure (fatal) destiny. Occurrence is "a spiral swerving towards a sphere of the sign, the simulacrum and simulation, a spiral of the reversibility of all signs in the shadow of seduction and death" (*EC* 79). Everything has lost its dialectical dimension and redoubles itself in ecstatic, transparent form (*FS* 43). That is: "Destiny is revealed within the mysterious sequence, the doubling of signs" (Gane 172). No longer is truth opposed by falsehood, but truth is opposed by a truth more true than true: "information processing"; the social is absorbed by the more social than social: "the masses"; and the real is presented as the more than real: "the hyperreal." The strategy of the object brings us to the point of saturation, to indeterminacy and relativism, and ultimately to cancerous hypertrophy (177). This site of overload Gane calls the "hypertelic," where opposition dissipates and becomes unrecognizable—a point of "hyperdetermination," hyperinertia, hyperreality, and hypereverything (176-177). Baudrillard treads through this passage to a new system, a new realm that appears destined, that is, "fatal." It is a mysterious point of no regress: "Only fatal strategies have any chance now of subverting the logic of this implosion: by hastening it or by perverting its own collapse" (Gane 65). Accosting the history of Enlightenment philosophy Baudrillard embraces Nietzschean nihilism:

> If the world is hardly compatible with the concept of the real which we impose upon it, the function of theory is certainly not to reconcile it, but on the contrary, to seduce, to wrest things from their condition, to force them into an over-existence which is incompatible with that of the real.... It must become simulation if it speaks about simulation, and deploy the same strategy as its object. If it speaks about seduction, theory must become the seducer, and deploy the same stratagems. If it no longer aspires to a discourse of truth, theory must assume the form of a world from which truth is withdrawn. And it thus becomes its very object. (*EC* 98)

Postmodern experience for Baudrillard is the entry into experiences of simulacra. To embrace any simulacrum requires us to leave everything that is "human" or "real"—to (dis)simulate and pass through the hyperreal.

It is here that Nietzsche's concept of the Overman might be summoned for a new postmodern culture dominated by the hyperreal and simulations. The Overman interprets difference in sameness, and can "will beyond." Nietzsche's "active forgetting" might make it possible to pass into a sort of "anti-metaphysics whose secret is that the masses (or Man) know with certainty that they don't need to pass judgment on themselves or the world, that they don't have to will, know, or desire" (*FS* 97). Reading Nietzsche and Baudrillard this way makes possible a new strategy, one that explores postmodern nihilism as the death of all the great referents (the Subject, the Social, the Real, etc.). Nihilism is not simply pessimism; it should be read, as Nietzsche once said, as "'a projection of the conditions of (our) preservation into the predicates of existence'" (qtd. in Cook and Kroker 183).

Kroker concludes that, following the Nietzschean trajectory, Baudrillard is *the* postmodern theorist, since his writing "is a kind of nihilistic simulation of the object itself in an attempt to reach its fundamental structures [cynical power, and dead capital] . . . it parades its truth in the form of catastrophic 'participation' in its object" (Gane 49). From this point on, Baudrillard renounces "any attempt to go beyond appearances to the unearthing of a latent structure from which it might be possible to read the world" (Gane 131). Henceforth, in Gane's view, the world/object must be approached in a radically new way (92). Our destiny is to side with the object, which is at the center of the world (*EC* 80). Gane adds: "it is no longer a question of producing a rational argument for a rational audience to consume by producing a replica of the 'real' as its truth, or of revealing it by tearing away its veils" (131). Baudrillard believes that in a world already seduced by the impossibility of Truth, Essence, or Objectivity, appearance is always victorious: "The present system of dissuasion and simulation succeeds in neutralizing all finalities, all referentials, all meanings, but it fails to neutralize appearances. It forcefully controls all the procedures for the production of meaning. It does not control the seduction of appearances. No interpretation can explain it, no system can abolish it. It is our last chance" (*EC* 74). Baudrillard's cultural theory responds to this phenomenon with a radical epistemological schism: If fatal theory has created a totally artificial and simulated space for existence, no longer containing reference points to an outside reality, we should enter the implosion. Surface, appearance, and seduction should be stressed against a fatal mastery of the world, the object, and meaning. What Baudrillard offers is a contemporary strategy of seduction. He writes in *Cool Memories* that the only seductive theory is "one in which concepts recede to infinity, lose themselves in features ever more extreme, lending themselves to indefinite paradox, to the point of inertia where conceptual emotion is engulfed in the discovery of a thousand pure signs, and the passion for their disappearance" (13).

Nietzsche's answer to nihilism was to express the "will to power" and to participate in the warring of Dionysian and Apollonian wills that is life: "blessing itself as that which must return eternally, as a becoming that knows no satiety, no disgust, no weariness" (*WP* 550). In a nihilistic universe reduced to a play of signs (the indeterminacy of infinitesimal signifiers) that never accedes to truth or meaning, Baudrillard's alternative is a strategy of seduction and appearances: "The capacity immanent to seduction to deny things their truth and turn it into a game, the pure play of appearances, and thereby foil all systems of power and meaning" (*SED* 8). For Baudrillard, in a world of simulation: "we are witnessing the slow and simultaneous erosion of all the polar structures [signifier/signified, truth/falsity, and reality/illusion], and the movement toward a universe that is losing the very dimension of meaning. Disinvested, disenchanted, and disaffected [signs]—we are experiencing the destiny of the world as will and representation" (*SED* 104). That is, the world of appearances forces us past Nietzsche into the "pure surface of events" and toward the "enchanted space of simulation" (*PI* 77), where human experience transforms the entire world into its image. This is a nihilistic logic, which is not simply pessimistic, but "makes our exterminism in the simulacrum an entirely satisfying condition for (our) preservation" (*PS* 130).

Chapter Three

Seduction, Radical Semiurgy, and the Logic of the Code

> What fascinates everyone is the debauchery of signs, that reality, everywhere and always, is debauched by signs.
>
> —Jean Baudrillard, *Fatal Strategies*

> Metaphysics wants a world of forms distinct from their doubles, their shadows, their images: this is the principle of Good. But the object is always the fetish, the false, the feticho, the factitious, the lure, everything that incarnates the abominable confusion of the thing with its magical and artificial double.
>
> —Jean Baudrillard, *Fatal Strategies*

Friedrich Nietzsche's epistemological skepticism prefigures our postmodern world of fetishized objects and Jean Baudrillard's call for seduction. Nietzsche described how humans are fatally compelled to move outside of subjectivity, via "truths," into the objective world. That is, humans set up systems of categorical "truths" by which it is believed an objective reality can be defined. In the process, however, we forget that these concepts themselves are already simulations, the chimeras of a perspectival will. This tendency to will fatally drives us to the object, whose destiny is always to be signed, and to seem ever-so familiar. The rationalist drive is our will to create an empirical world, but this action only takes place to the extent that humanity can see or describe the world as metaphor or sign—insofar as humanity can represent the empirical world of objects by imposing its own logic. Our fault is to believe that the referent precedes the sign: "on the contrary, reality is the effect of the sign" (*EDOI* 47). Our experience of reality is that of an imaginary and subjective construct—an orbital set of references, or signs, which are imposed upon the occurring world, organizing it into an always already existing system of signification. As Nietzsche has said: "How should explanations be at all possible when we first turn everything into an image, our image!" (*GS* 172).

Nietzsche and Baudrillard both recognize a world in which image (the illusion of form) always precedes the imperfect world of simulations that can only follow—the world in which the real has always already been seduced, captured by the image. For Baudrillard humanity can't escape the world of appearances: "*Even before being produced, the world was seduced. A strange precession which today still weighs on all reality*" (*FS* 183). The problem is that from the beginning, the "reality" of the world has been tainted by the illusion that the world can move to greater exactitude (*EDOI* 44). In our existent world, the real is always already signed, systematized, and modeled—these linguistic structures (metaphors) convert "becoming" into "being," and on the screen, convert "real" into "image." In operation is the precession of simulacra, in which the destiny of the "real" is always to occur in simulation (death). It is a continuous implosion by which any "difference" is eclipsed by "same" to be simulacra. Everything is sacrificially doubled into signs, and then "redoubled" in its fatal occurrence: "As it is thus necessary to develop from prediction to prophesy, and this is the order of destiny, the world is comprehensible only as a precession and return of the sign" (Gane 172).

In our postmodern experiences there is no longer any "original" experience, only return, redoubling. In redoubling, it is the destiny of an image to exponentially unfold into perspectival space—an unfolding of images with which the world must somehow keep up in a deadly pace of realization (signing and passing). In this implosion between image and event, the energy of the real is engulfed by simulation. Modern media have brought about a fatal paradox concerning the exponential multiplying of images: the world has become truly infinite (*EDOI* 29-30). At this point of "realization" of infinite representations and meanings, the hyperreal is reached. Now, images become the basis for the real itself. "The very definition of the real has become: that of which it is possible to give an equivalent reproduction.... The real is not only what can be reproduced, but that which is always already reproduced; that is, the hyperreal ... which is entirely simulation" (*SIM* 146). In the space of the hyperreal, the image coincides absolutely with reality. In this motion, the real is replaced with the idea of the world as pure simulation. *Day One* is a television series in which media events happen as a made-for-TV serial, much like the "real" evening (or CNN) news these days, or the O. J. Simpson trial. In a world where reality is modeled on appearances, reality "appears," or occurs, as simulation (hence, the disappearance of the real into signs and images). How many children's first experiences of a harvest moon were already defined for them on TV by McDonald's "Mac at Night" commercials? Today, it seems one must continually discern: "Is it live, or is it MEMOREX?"

Nietzsche foretold that it would be our fate to live through a process of reversal of the real. Today many of us find ourselves confronted with the loss of the illusion of the real and the disappearance of reality into hyperreality. The reality of the world has always been its illusion, the symbolic play of signs and referents, and the subsequent loss of the power to exert illusion is perilous. According to Baudrillard: "Illusion is no longer possible. It has always braked the real, but now no longer holds; and we are witness to the unfurling of the real in a world without illusions . . . the real has become the rational. This conjunction has been realized under the sign of the hyperreal, ecstatic form of the real" (*FS* 71). By trying to possess the real world through rational forms and scientific development, we have abolished it for the ecstatic logic of the hyperreal. The nature of reality, which has always been only "apparent," is now based on statistical models, computer simulations, television imagery, and consumer polls: "In short, what we have now is a principle of non-reality based on reality'—a principle of 'hyperreality'" (*EDOI* 51).

Like Nietzsche's work, Baudrillard's tends to conclude that, since the Renaissance, rationalism in science and in art has experienced a series of catastrophic consequences for the Western world. The fatal strategies of reason and rationality do not make meaning or significance, but lead to neutralization and break "the cycle of appearances" (Gane 171). Kroker likewise comments on the subversion: "Here, in a big ontological flip, techno-culture is materialized—*form* comes alive—and Baudrillard is a radical empiricist studying *our* implosion in the violent semiurgy of 'rationalist eschatology'" (*PI* 57). Nietzsche had pointed out that, through rationalist thought, both the world of reality and appearances have disappeared: "[when] 'we have abolished the real world; what world is left? the apparent world perhaps? . . . But no! *with the real world we have also abolished the apparent world!*'" (*Twilight of the Idols* 41). Today, the difference between appearance and depth is collapsing from both sides. Brian Singer describes this as follows:

> Consider first the appearances collapsing into reality. Suppose the enlightenment dream is being realized and we are living in an increasingly transparent society, a society without secrets or areas of darkness, without veils, blinders or illusions, a society where what was hidden is becoming visible and all that is visible is, as a result, becoming substantial. It would be a society where all appearances would be real, equally real and, accordingly, equally unreal. . . . Now consider the other side of the coin, reality

collapsing into appearance. Suppose the appearances substitute themselves for the underlying reality and become that by which we gauge what is "truly real" in place of (or in the absence of) any real functioning referent. In this case one has moved beyond a world of verisimilitude, where appearances appear real, into a world of simulation, where appearances appear more real than reality—what Baudrillard calls the "hyper-real"—because "reality" as we experience it is modelled on appearances (rather than appearances being modelled on reality). Again one confronts a society of appearances (in the form of simulated models), where appearances are "real" and "reality" (as expressed in the hyper-real) appears as the most significant of "illusions." (141)

In both cases, reality (dis)appears.

In a world where "reality" and appearance continually collapse into each other, "reality" can only be discussed as a "world from which truth has been withdrawn" (*EC* 98). Along with Nietzsche, one should recognize the "truth" of appearances. Christopher Norris asserts that if Baudrillard is right: "any attempt to get at the truth behind appearances, or lay bare the sophistries that maintain this illusion—is necessarily a mistaken and dangerous endeavor" (174). For Baudrillard, indeed, such an attempt is nothing short of insanity: "From where could there have originated the crazy idea of revealing the secret, exposing the bare substance, touching radical obscenity? . . . There is no real, there never was a real. Seduction knows this and preserves its enigma" (*FS* 108). Acknowledging Nietzsche's diagnosis of nihilism, Baudrillard claims there is *nothing* behind appearances, and this must remain a secret (*SED* 94).

Historically, our critical efforts have been to annul the significance of artifice, or seduction, and "to abolish the mystery of the veil" (Gane 145). The major consequence is the destruction of the symbolic order and the introduction of the "real world" (201). The symbolic universe is the "shimmering fabric of signs" (Ross 216), a system of play that offers the illusion of the real. To remove the symbolic layer is to destroy the illusion that it maintains. In a symbolic universe "the power of signs lies in their appearance and disappearance; that is how they efface the world" (*SED* 94). Baudrillard has stated: "The symbolic is neither a concept, an agency, a category, nor a 'structure,' but an act of exchange and *a social relation which puts an end to the real*" (*SE&D* 133). Baudrillard moves toward a critique based on symbolic exchange as an epistemology—not of a system based on production/consumption and signifiers/signifieds but on seduction, challenges, equivalences, and reciprocities. As Baudrillard has said: "One could conceive of a theory dealing with signs, terms, and values on the basis of their seductive attraction, and not in terms of their contrast or calculated opposition" (*EC* 58).

Thus, Baudrillard sets out to work in the symbolic, which he sees as the enemy of the metaphysics of the sign and complicit with the play of seduction and appearances. "*Seduction represents mastery over the symbolic universe, while power represents only mastery of the real universe*" (*SED* 8). Indifference and ambivalence are seductive aspects of what Baudrillard terms *symbolic exchange*. In this vein, Stephen Pfohl writes: "In symbolic exchange, ambivalence challenges 'the false transparency of the sign'" (171). Baudrillard uses the following example to explain the necessity to maintain seduction (the game of appearances): "Take for example the story of the woman to whom a man sends an ardent love letter. She asks him what part of her seduced him the most.... Her eyes, of course. And he receives in the mail, wrapped in brown paper, the woman's eye.... Literalizing the metaphor, she abolishes the symbolic order. The sign becomes the thing" (*BL* 110). It is this sort of transparency, where the sign functions so purely that one enters the ludic universe of Baudrillard.

In the *Ecstasy of Communication*, Baudrillard discusses the consequential end of metaphysics and the beginning of the hyperreal: "that which was previously mentally projected, which was lived as metaphor in the terrestrial habitat is from now on projected, entirely without metaphor, into the absolute space of simulation" (*EC* 16). Television, in which signs lose their real world referents, is the prime example of this. TV never sends us back to the real but serves as a self-referential medium for the replacement of lived experiences. Television reaches an extreme point of nihilism in which "[a]ll that was metaphor has already materialized, collapsed into reality" (*FS* 70). Or, one could say that everything on television (which is without depth) occurs in the "hyperealized" form of TV and advertising imagery (*BL* 69). In this hyperreality, the (depthless) object serves as nothing more than the pure site of representation, as a simulated will. Individuals are driven toward seeing the world as a pure object, where all objects are destined to operate as blank screens upon which simulacra can operate. Look at the advertising simulacra in which the image is attached to the product with no determinable significance: Golden Flake potato chips (quite naturally) appear as mountains in one commercial and as the space shuttle in another. Sumo wrestlers perform high dives in a Miller Lite beer advertisement. This is a purely relational space where the exchange of the sign is substituted for pure simulation: "[W]ho could say what the reality is that these signs simulate? ... The cool universe of digitality has absorbed the world of metaphor and metonym. The principle of simulation wins out over the reality principle just as over the principle of pleasure" (*SIM* 152). Even more frightening is the exchange of "war" for its hyperreal depiction as news, miniseries, or entertainment (TV cameras awaited the Marines on the shores of Somalia).

The phase of Baudrillard's work on seduction concerns his analysis of the (fatal) destiny of the world as pure object (moving toward death, signs, resemblance, and simulation). Where illusion is no longer possible (having entered hyperreality, the ecstatic form of the real) indifference rules the universe. As Mike Gane contends, experience ceases to be dialectical and becomes destiny: "comprehensible only as the precession and return of the sign ... the ceremony of the world follows the same order" (172). Like Nietzsche, Baudrillard realizes the tenuous and ineluctable situation of the "always already"—that there is no detour because the entire system operates by destiny—so that individuals must somehow operate from within the language of enchantment and seduction. Whereas Nietzsche stresses the affirmation of life (will) against death (simulacrum), Baudrillard proceeds to connect simulation with seduction. If simulation precedes the real, then humans must learn to live in simulation—we must side with the object (*FS* 190).

For Baudrillard, this side of objects is the feminine metaphor, the side of "woman" that "seduces." In *Spurs*, Jacques Derrida remarks on the complicity between the woman and seduction as comprehending all the "veiling effects" of life (51). Seduction is a strategy of appearances (Gane 147). A woman is always in the realm of appearance: "since she is a model for truth [Nietzschean, as totally *apparent*], she is able to display the gifts of her seductive power" (*Spurs* 67). A woman is both superficial and authentic—that is, she is authentic in her artificiality. The feminine "where the distinction between authenticity and artifice is without foundation, also defines the space of simulation" (*SED* 11). In a phallogocentric culture, women are always already forced into an order of simulation: "In order to speak, to represent herself, a woman assumes a masculine position; perhaps this is why femininity is frequently associated with masquerade, with false representation, with simulation and seduction" (Owens 59). Thus, the "feminine" is simulation, for "femininity provides radical evidence of simulation and the only possibility of its overcoming—in seduction precisely" (*SED* 11). In this capacity a woman serves as the "ruin of representation," as Michele Montrelay proposes (qtd. in Owens 59).

Nietzsche was the first to recognize the fatal outcome of the seductive forces that would have to be played out when he wrote: "Ja, das Leben ist ein Weib!" For Nietzsche, "truth is like a woman" as Derrida notes (*Spurs* 51). Woman, as "veil," as "simulation," is "but one name for that untruth of truth" (*Spurs* 51). The image provoked by a woman is that there is no Truth (and this she keeps secret). "Woman" conceals herself behind Schein and Schonheit, her "capacity for deception." The very idea of "woman" suggests the apparent qualities of aversion, (non)essentialness, distance, and appearance, which, paradoxically, are truth. In her multiplicity and superficiality, truth (as only apparent) returns to woman: "Truth can only be surface," Derrida contends (*Spurs* 59). The phallogocentric tradition of rationalism wants to impose metaphors for Truth (presence and totalities) on women. Zarathustra declares: "'Woman, give me your little truth'" and the old woman replies: "'You are going to women? Do not forget the whip'" (*Spurs* 67). Men bring their whips (phalluses) by which to impose their wills upon that which always (comp)lies and seduces (woman, power, and the object). Men create "truths" in their values. As a woman "obeys" (or deceives), much like the object in Baudrillard, women remain truth in (dis)simulation (*Spurs* 53). In (dis)simulation, the woman knows that "truth" (as perspectival) is always already imbued with masculine interpretation.

Postmodern nihilism marks the "transition from signs which (dis)simulate something to signs which (dis)simulate that there is nothing" (*SIM* 12). Baudrillard reasons: "To (dis)simulate is to feign not to have what one has. To simulate is to feign to have what one hasn't. One implies a presence, the other an absence" (*SIM* 5). Simulation is always "signed" by the lack, the absence, and the aporias of logocentrism. The "presence" (or truth) of "woman" is that, in (dis)simulation, she can always feign anything—that she always already feigned. In her superficiality, a woman feigns not to have the truth. As the major allegory of Truth in phallogocentrism, what has been associated with "woman" is always already a simulation of the masculine (nihilistic) will. The obscenity of postmodernity may be the loss of seduction and the "feminine" (Gane 151). Seduction, or the power of the feminine, might sustain the collapse of difference. In the same way, the maternal truth (dis)simulates and preserves itself as the mother tongue. The "feminine" (dis)simulates as truth, and that permits her to be the eternal life-giving force. The "masculine" is the signing, the death, the return. In simulacrum (the return of difference as same), Being robs "becoming" of difference. This is the order of the masculine, the double. Like a woman, the object seduces in that it knows it is always already simulating a masculine (rational) Truth. The feminine is always in the realm of appearances; it is not in the order of production. Nor is it the opposite of the masculine, since it is what "seduces the masculine" form of experiences (*SED* 7). The feminine (anti-essential and contradictory) may be the only way beyond male power (that which is empty or cynical). Baudrillard insists: "seduction, by producing only illusions, obtains all powers, including the power to return [a masculine] production and reality to their fundamental illusion" (*SED* 70).

Our postmodern world presents the abandonment of seduction and "the feminine" as a loss of illusion. In this system, everything thought to freely exist becomes the object in its return as the simulacrum of something that has preceded it—the world as a pure object upon which the rationalist will is imposed, or a pure screen onto which infinite perspectives project and to which all experiences are leveled. A Nietzchean affirmation of "difference" gives way to a willing of the "same." This state of affairs is obscene! Baudrillard suggests that in this new "obscenity": "Illusion is no longer valid here: it is truth which bursts into free expression. We are all actors and spectators; there is no more stage; the stage is everywhere; no more rules: everyone plays out his own drama improvising on his own fantasies" (*FS* 63). In postmodern society, the stage is in the process of being swept away to make room for the pure empty form of the real—just watch *Big Brother*, *Real Sex* or *Cops* to see. There is no longer any distance between reality and appearance—an obscene proximity of all events has taken hold: "Everywhere a stage disappears, and everywhere the poles that sustained intensity or difference are stricken with inertia" (*FS* 63).

The (ob)scene, the terror of hypervisiblity, has the power to strip everything of its appearance and to exterminate seduction, leaving a perfectly ecstatic universe of pure objects (as signs) and resemblances (*FS* 60). "Everything obscene is a matter of surface" (*FS* 65). It is no longer the illusion of a represented real but is now only the unfolding of surface as the real, representing nothing at all. Baudrillard tells us: "There is no longer transcendence, but the immanent surface of development of operations, smooth surface, operational, of communication. . . . As with television, the entire surrounding world, and our own bodies, become a control screen" (*FS* 66). Baudrillard considers the obscenity of the world to be a pure object that

> starts when there is no longer a scene when everything becomes inexorably transparent. . . . Not only the sexual becomes obscene in pornography, today there's a whole pornography of information and communication, circuits and networks, a pornography of functions and objects in their readability, fluidity, availability, regulation polyvalence, compulsory meaning, free expression. . . . This is the obscenity of what is entirely soluble in communication. (*FS* 67-68)

As illusion is given up to transparency, one discovers the total circulation of all codes. The object is now the space or screen upon which "information" imposes truth—the social upon which polls inscribe facts, the world on which reality is imposed. It is not the site where the subject represents the object; in an ironic reversal, the object simulates the subject's will purely. As modern culture and its objects pass into a system of signs (the perspectival illusion), the subject is ultimately "dominated by the system of objects (interpreted as signs) which constitute our everyday life" (Kellner 9). An object equivocates with the proliferation of signs that transform life (as artifice or nontruth) into simulacrum (screenal image or information).

For Baudrillard, the "evil" principle of the object is precisely that it is indifferent, obedient, and transparent (*FS* 182). The object (though impenetrable), challenges the subject that insists on entering a fully ironic surface relation: "This is why [the object] shows—mischievously, diabolically—its voluntary servitude; bends willingly, like nature, to any law we impose upon it" (*FS* 182). The subject is seduced by the object, which is "immanent and enigmatic"—"a good conductor of the fatal" (Gane 174). The conspiring object of fatal theory "*is considered more cunning, cynical, talented than the subject, for which it lies in wait*" (*FS* 181). Destiny is the force of all fatal strategies. Gane holds that: "The object plays the game, it redoubles it, outbidding strategic constraints, in a strategy which does not have its own ends or objectives, but induces the subject into a fatal logic" (176). The danger, Gane points out, is to be caught on the side of the subject (from its point of view). There are two processes at work here, according to Gane:

> Banal strategies are those that emanate from the subject, and are posed with all the superiorities of the subject in its apparent mastery of the

world. . . . But for a fatal strategy it is assumed that the subject as object is more subtle, more ingenious, than the subject. . . . But objective irony works through the very passionate *indifference* [italics mine] of the object, and this has a unique form of violation of the symbolic order. It is precisely diabolical as it leans towards the subject and seduces it. (174)

One can perceive in these relations the tension between masculine subjectivity and feminine seduction (as object). The anti-essentialist position of the feminine could be advantageous in this scenario.

Baudrillard presents us with the subject's effort to become the object that easily serves as the site of seduction. Seduction operates by indifference and homogenization. Douglas Kellner comments: "Banal strategies involve belief in referents such as the subject, power, revolution, the real, desire and so on, which Baudrillard believes have disappeared" (160). Fatal strategies pass to the side of the object, where the subject is no longer sovereign. The subject itself becomes the object as it "wills" its entire "being" in the world. It is what Baudrillard describes as the reversal of the terrorism of the subject against the object (Gane 174). The language of seduction is immanently reversible between the subject and the object: "If everything finally disobeys the symbolic order, it's because everything was subverted from the very beginning" (*FS* 183). As the subject dies, we pass to the side of the object: "When I speak of the object and its fatal strategies, I'm speaking also of people and their inhuman strategies" (*FS* 184). The object now fascinates and seduces us, in the form of commodities, fashion, the media, information, and models (Kellner 157). When Baudrillard speaks of the object, however, he is "referring to all of us and to our social and political order" (*SW* 199).

As it becomes clear that the methods of Enlightenment philosophy have represented a nihilistic power imposing its will upon the world, one begins to see from the side of the object. Baudrillard reasons: "perhaps the subject will see itself one day seduced by its object (which is quite natural), and it will become once more the prey of appearance" (*FS* 82). The side of seduction is the side of the object that (dis)simulates within the simulacrum that poses as the thing-in-itself. To seduce is to manipulate "appearances." Today, truth—or significance—can only be sought in the realm of appearance and seduction. Before simulation, art could seduce the reality of things; after simulation, the universe becomes "disenchanted" (*EDOI* 52). For example, consider the metafiction of television and writing, and the parody in art that calls attention to itself as artifice—there is no longer any illusion to things, and also there is no longer a reality, but hyperreality, and it is found everywhere from scholarly journals to television commercials. The problem is that these strategies lead us to indifference. The effect is discerned when one tries to distinguish "real" violence from simulation in *Dirty Harry* movies, Keystone Cop cartoons, the series *Cops*, the CNN Gulf War, and the Rodney King beating on the *CBS*

Evening News. The meaning of "violence" degenerates into the hyperreal experience of its depiction in images. How, otherwise, could the "real cops" who beat Rodney King be found innocent? Moreover, why is "real" violence allowed to proliferate on our streets? Do many of us desire the hyperreality it enjoys on the screen? The oscillation between real and simulated violence is the obscene instance of a truly abject social form of spectacle participation.

The loss of seduction and the end of illusion is the obscenity of the hyperreal (Gane 152). As Baudrillard asserts, we must be protected from the disastrous consequences of the real by maintaining our artificial fetish for appearances: "For God knows where unleashed meaning would lead to when it refuses to reproduce itself as appearance" (*FS* 186). On the other hand, to move beyond a world of appearances into the hyperreal is dangerous, like entering the schizophrenic's reality, in which the world lacks distance and difference: "[T]he schizophrenic cannot produce the limits of his very being.... He becomes a pure screen, a pure absorption and resorption surface of the influent networks" (*EC* 27). This might explain mass murderers' fascination with the celebratory nature of their crimes (the evening news, TV movies, trading cards, documentaries, etc.). The immanent surface connection of all meaning, this exteriorization of the entire world by obscene overexposure to media events, is recognized as a schizophrenic experience:

> The schizo is deprived of all scene, open to all in spite of himself, and in the greatest confusion. He is himself obscene, the obscene prey of the world's obscenity. What characterizes him is less his light-years distance from the real, a radical break, than absolute proximity, with no retreat; end of interiority and intimacy, overexposure and transparency of the world that transverses him without his being able to interpose any barrier. (*FS* 70)

In the postmodern world, lacking distance or interiority, where everything occurs instantaneously and is explicitly visible, there is no longer space for the hidden or obscure. For Baudrillard, as for Nietzsche: "Only artifice can dispel this lack of differentiation, this coupling of same to same" (*FS* 51). Seduction is a game that must be willed—Nietzsche's "will to will." Baudrillard writes: "*To seduce is to die as reality and reconstitute oneself as illusion*" (*SED* 67). When speaking of the seduction of Disneyland, Baudrillard refered to it as the necessary bunker of the real (a site of pure representation) that maintains the illusion that the outside world of appearances is itself reality (*SIM* 25).

As the collapse of opposition (e.g., appearance/reality and truth/illusion) makes the obscene equivalency of all things obvious, surface and seduction can be stressed against a mastery of the world, the object, and meaning. Seduction (more false than false) diverts us from Truth. As Nietzsche believed, one must deny the possibility of a Truthful world. Truth exists in the empty circulation of signs on the surface (where difference is put into forms). For Baudrillard, it is necessary to quit the "real world" of Truths and totally admit to the world of seductions and of nontruths—Nietzsche's world of "apparent lies." When the "madman" runs into the market decrying (in response to rationalism) that "God is dead," he asks: "What festivals of atonement, what sacred games shall we have to invent?" (*GS* 181). In a world where images and appearances are becoming reality, individuals must "will to" seduction, games, and primitive rituals, because, as Singer asserts: "games do not have an external truth: their "truth" is entirely immanent, which is to say they know neither truth nor falsehood" (144). Singer describes this process thus: "In other words, the world of truth, reality, production, law and desire is shadowed by a parallel world of appearance, illusion, seduction and games which can be exalted in a manner both forceful and ironic by virtue of its logical autonomy" (146).

Facing the fatal logic of postmodernism head on, Baudrillard is interested in carrying our "new situation to its very limits" (*BL* 131). Arthur Kroker attributes to postmodernism: "The anesthetization of experience to such a point of excess that nature, subjectivity, and desire migrate into seduction: into a game of chance and indifferent relations of pure positionality" (*PI* 5). Baudrillard's "seduction," as a challenge, parallels Nietzsche's "dance" and ludic "laughter," and Giles Deleuze and Felix Guattari's schizo equation. To seduce is to play in appearances and bring about (mis)interpretations that challenge the technological will to power of a New World Order as a capitalist simulacrum. Seduction, then, occurs as the possibility for a world "in which everything appears and disappears in accordance with an incessant cycle of metamorphoses with the seductive (not rational) chains of forms and appearance" (Morris 204). Embracing seduction, one must actively (mis)interpret to affirm life in simulation (more true than true), hyperreality (deserted forms of the real—TV) and cynical signs (the death of denotation)—a universe that "must be interpreted in terms of play, challenges, duels, the strategy of appearances—that is, the terms of seduction" (*SED* 7). There is only one fate worse than death for Baudrillard—"the fatal illness of those who can never be seduced" (Morris 190).

Baudrillard's thought traces the postmodern implosion of the real into a fully nihilistic society of signs. We live in the age of a massive semiological cancellation, in the "presence of a sign-system which functions on the basis of the liquidation of the real" (*PS* 115). More and more we try to "(real)ize" every desire in the production of signs. But "the real" remains only that which is represented—the lack never recuperated in the "process," the incomplete movement that reproduces itself (in sign form) every time it tries to overcome the signifying gap. Here, everything wants to be exchanged: reality for image, sign for signified, and the flesh for consciousness (*PS* 79). As Kroker claims: "the division of the order of signs from the immediacy of corporeal existence" means that carnal experience is given up (*PS* 75). All representational (nihilistic) experience is caught in the exchange of the real (life) for the sign (death). How else might one explain the popularity of the B-movie actor Ronald Reagan as president, whose very "presence" was a stage show, a slogan, or a script prepared by media consultants (Potter 24)? On another front, why go to Germany when Busch Gardens: "The Old Country" in Williamsburg, Virginia, has it all there for you without the hassle of international travel? It's just the same, from authentic Hofbrau Hauser serving German beers and sauerkraut to the room in a Holiday Inn at which you would stay. In late-capitalism, whole cultures are exchanged as commodities.

Today, representational space has moved into simulated space. Baudrillard's universe is simply one in which "simulation neutralizes the poles [referent/sign, truth/falsity, and world/metaphor] that organize perspectival space of the real" (*SED* 155). In postmodern culture, the individual enters into a simulacral proliferation of signs, codes, and the triumph of simulation (a real more real than the real), where (hyper)reality is ascribed more to signs and images than to things. It is a semiological continent where the social and the real are all given over to simulation. Television is the supreme force in this logic of exterminism. The telematic proliferation of signs collapses the difference between media and reality, so that ultimately the real world is traded in against a simulacrum. Baudrillard goes so far as to suggest that "this process constitutes a significant reversal of the relation between representation and reality. Previously the media were believed to mirror, reflect, represent reality, whereas now they are coming to constitute a (hyper)reality, a new media reality, 'more real than the real,' where 'the real' is subordinate to representation thus leading ultimately to a dissolving of the real" (qtd. in Kellner 68). In all facets of life, real experiences have been replaced with representations and simulations, from computers that do our thinking for us, to TV that replaces any need to experience the "real thing." In fact, TV always happens as if "it" is the real thing, and the screen runs continuously from the event taking place into our own living room (the baseball game during which persons cheer for the home run as if they were there, or the O. J. Simpson pursuit viewed in unison with millions of others who are simultaneously "tuned in"). Baudrillard describes a postmodern culture in which radical semiurgy (in the form of a proliferation of signs and meanings, or media images and messages) produces simulations and simulacra that in turn create new social forms of experience and subjectivity. There is no longer the scene and mirror apart from the subject; the object no longer mirrors the subject's desire (*EC* 12). Now, everything transpires as if it were part of a massive television screen or computer network: it is no longer necessary to project ourselves into it like a video game because we are virtually part of it. Our entire public and private lives seemingly unfold as monitoring screens in continuous interplay with a network of communications (*EC* 16).

Baudrillard's major hypothesis in *In the Shadow of the Silent Majorities* is that the space of the social is now that of simulation (*PS* 173). The processing of the real (and the social) into a sign system (cybernetic, digital, and telecommunicative) implodes into the simulacrum of cynical (empty) power. Unlike Michel Foucault's account of power, through the contemporary proliferation of signs: "power comes to reside in codes, simulations, media and the like, rather than in actual institutional forces and relations" (Kellner 133). That is to say, the social is one among many "truth-effects" of a neutralizing (as opposed to normalizing) power (*PS* 173). The postmodern condition is one in which we have already passed the vanishing point of representational power where the connections between sign and referent remained, by necessity, distinct: "Power, in this case, always stood for something *real* outside itself: a referent like use-value, sovereignty, justice, democracy which would, and this simultaneously, concretize the regression into nothingness in the will to power" (*PS* 114). For Baudrillard, power operates as a mirage, a layer of signs under which nothing exists (Kellner 139). Think again of President Ronald Reagan's political staging. Kroker adds: "Having no existence 'in itself' this is a power that takes on the *simulated* life of a changing order of significations. Power/sex, power/norm, power/grace, power/knowledge, power/sign" (*PS* 103).

Baudrillard's account of the social mechanisms of power is not the normalizing power/society of Foucault. For Foucault, power (re)produces itself at every moment, at every point—it is not a thing, but is disseminated everywhere (in literature, social norms, religious doctrines, and ideological discourses). Here, power is relational, a dynamic of control and lack of control between discourses and subject—putting into discourse the movements, the behavior, and the manifestations of the subject. For example, *The History of Sexuality* looks at how the polymorphous techniques and transfiguration of power, such as social power relations, are produced and sustained (transcribed against the body) in the discursive production of sexuality. On the other hand, power, for Baudrillard, no longer simply resides in discourses and institutions but is even more abstract, being dispersed throughout society by the media and appearing as simulation. To describe the condition, Pfohl writes:

> Following Baudrillard it may now be necessary to ask whether the media infestation of a great many of our HIStorical embodiments has advanced to such a state-in-excess that many of us are no longer manipulated externally like robots but are being materially accessed by the fascinating (if panicky) inFORMational vectors of ultramodern CAPITAL itself. Here we may find ourselves struggling adrift and swimming within the fast, dense, technologically relayed wavelengths of new forms of power; seduced and/or abandoned to the point of actually taking the telecommunicative media within ourselves; its inFORMational screens and its terminals now ritually functioning as if our most intimate organs of sensation, erasing previously imagined difference between the public and private, the personal and political, the cognitive and carnal. (21)

Postmodern power is power on the reverse side—where power affirms itself as absence in its redoubling as simulacrum (*PS* 117).

The result, within our postmodern society, is a semiological proliferation in which empty signs of a cynical power simulate "a void, which seeks to embody itself in the 'reality-effects' of human speech and social action" (*PS* 116), so as to "appear" as the "real thing." The television camera saturates us with images of President Bill Clinton waving to an approving crowd. Individuals unwittingly participate in their surveillance by every possible data bank (social security numbers, credit card histories, phone listings, etc.). The Gulf War was played across the globe on CNN depicting the technological image of the New World Order that will follow America's lead. What PR; what "power"! As if to celebrate the event, Kroker writes: "Foucault has said that power in the postmodern era could only function on the condition that it hide its (real) existence as purely cynical (*PS* 114) . . . which consists only of plunging downwards through endlessly refracted imagery" (*PS* 115). The media play an important role in this "refraction" of power as a "simulation machine which reproduces images, signs and codes which in turn come to constitute an autonomous realm of (hyper)reality and [consequently] . . . the obliteration of the social" (Kellner 68). This site of obliteration occurs where the social is processed into a sign system that appears as information. The social (as the fatal object of the technocracy) is transformed into a simulated form, a "black hole" of information absorption. How many polls are there that express public opinion?

As simulation, the social is no longer meaningful. That is, it no longer expresses meaning since it is reduced (by surveys, studies, tests, etc.) to a "mass" of information and message processing. The logic (of code) which dominates the masses is that of digitality, an order of connections and electronic impulses that comes to organize social life. Instead of "real" social relations, such interactions are mediated through electronic circuits and computer networks. (So many of us rely on e-mail and answering machines for communication.) Baudrillard conceives of the social contract now as a pact of coded significations by which individuals are emulsified and seduced into participation (simulation) through communication and information networks (computer, media, telephone, etc.). He sees "communication as the functioning of the social within a closed circuit, where signs duplicate an undiscoverable reality. The social contract has become a 'simulation pact' sealed by the media and the news" (*SED* 162). Go no further than the Gulf War to find a mediatized experience that all levels of society might share in the same hypnotic way, with the same military-induced "spins" and the same corporate-controlled sponsorship. Or, take, for example, the hyperreality of the news events on November 22, 1963, which were rebroadcast perfectly, to the minute, for each of us to relive on that same date in 1993. Even those who weren't born yet when the event "really" occurred could experience that apotheosis of obscenity, the event of total (dis)illusionment in America marked by the obscene (now ever-present) moment at which an entire nation simultaneously entered the implosion of postmodernity. Just like The Gulf War saga, The Hyperreal Kennedy Assassination occurs as a simulated event, where reality explodes into the commercialization of infinite theories, perspectives, and "truths."

For Baudrillard, the media and technology combine to produce a new social order: a "'cyberblitz' whereby individuals, objects and society are subjected to the effects of cybernetic codes, models, and modulations and the steering systems of a society which aims at perfecting its instruments of social control" (Kellner 77). Foucault's society of surveillance becomes, for Baudrillard, a society of "simulation codes." Media, fashion, and consumerism—all domains of social life—are programmed, so that everyday life takes place by design. As Kellner explains: "the codes send signals and continually test individuals, inscribing them into the simulated order. Responses are structured in a binary system of affirmation or negation: every ad, fashion, commodity, television program, political candidate and poll presents a test to which one is to respond" (80). In postmodern society "the model or code structures social reality and erodes distinctions between the model and the real" (63). In a hyperreality that exists in the transparent logic of the code, the play of indeterminate signs and images replaces reality: "At this level, the question of signs and their rational destination; their *real* and their *imaginary*; their repression; their reversal; the illusions they sketch . . . all of these are swept from the table" (*SW* 140). When the distinction between reality and imagination is effaced, when the real vanishes into our system of images and signs, everything becomes "undecidable," or neutral and indifferent, and what emerges is "the domination of the free-flowing code" (*SW* 128). The indeterminacy of the code finds its pinnacle in an electronic media that has made perspective proliferate in signs, thus making them infinitely irreal (i.e., they exchange exclusively among themselves without interacting with the real). As Kellner points out: "in a world of commodity signs, media spectacles, representations and simulations, . . . there is no longer any access to a 'real' which is itself presented as an effect of the code or system" (64). Everything simply occurs as preceded by the programming of a circulatory code (fashion for designer lifestyles, DNA as biological control, etc.). For Baudrillard "the order of ends has ceded its place to molecular play, as the order of signifieds has yielded to the play of infinitesimal signifiers, condensed into their aleatory commutation" (*SE&D* 59). Thus, as our human existence increasingly merges with models of simulation, we live in an entirely relativistic and indeterminable universe of signs, images, and information coding leading beyond a sphere of interpretation into tyrannical simulation (Kellner 64).

Today, individuals are confronted with a digital world of information processing and cynical signs that circulate telematically by the logic of late-capitalist code. Kroker writes: "In the discourse of a power which is structured as a 'perspectival appearance,' symbolism and materiality coalesce only to be vaporized into a pure nothingness. Everything is to be reduced to the new universal exchange-principle of information" (*PS* 74). Technological advancement is the historical nexus of Nietzsche and Baudrillard at which point the real, transformed into information, disappears into its equivalent: the computer model, the matrices of a statistical study, or the image on television (*SIM* 2-3). The model is always made "in its own image," and awaits "realization" in simulation. Here, again, is the loss of "difference" between real and simulation—"A hyperreal henceforth sheltered from the imaginary, leaving room only for the orbital recurrence of models and the simulated generation of difference" (*SIM* 4). At this point, signs and images increasingly refer, not to an outside reality, but only to other signs and images in the system. Such a system of equivalence that substitutes signs of the real for the real itself has no further need for the production of the real. The double becomes that which is truer than true, and the dialectical progression from referent to image (that of materially "producing" reality in the "positivity" of the sign) may fail to operate: "The new order is an immense game, where all values are equalized and can be exchanged in a cross-societal leveling.... The referent, 'reality', as a basis for the production of distinction is abolished: 'the signifier becomes its own referent'"(Gane 111). In hyperreality, all references are always already only to other simulacra—representation, the real, and reproduction are all the "same." A tour of Universal Studios in Orlando will confirm this, since in this place experience is always already of the order of simulation, not only in the case of movies simulating real life, but in the case of movies as real life. At Universal Studios patrons "ride the movies," where the movies are reality and we are their characters. Universal Studios is a hyperreality in which the movies are the real world. In this "universe": "[h]yperrealism is made an integral part of a coded reality that it perpetuates, and for which it changes nothing" (*SIM* 147). This is a system of a "gigantic simulacrum—not unreal, but yet a simulacrum, never again exchanging for what is real, but exchanging in itself, in an uninterrupted circuit without reference or circumference" (*SIM* 11). In the hyperreality of Universal Studios the apparent truth of simulation itself empties into the state of being a simulacrum. Movies, as representations of real life, empty into real-life simulations of movies—not real movies being filmed, but the simulation of real movies, where a member of the audience "is" Norman Bates on the (replica) set of *Psycho* and is inserted into the movie and played on the screen, while a film of Anthony Perkins tells us how to "really" play the scene. This sort of reflexivity, in which reality is transformed into simulation (the audience sees itself watching a simulation of the movie on the screen), reproduces a cultural logic of simulation characterized by an indifference to differences between reality and representation (Denzin 11-12).

At this point of saturation, reality loses out to the image. Hyperreality "must be read as a triumph of the code of a general equivalence of all things, the increasing possibility of sign exchanges of all realities" (Gane 112). Look at today's commercials in which the images no longer produce a signifier/signified relationship. A bag of Golden Flake potato chips sails the ocean as a windsurfer's mast in one ad and lifts off as the space shuttle's engines in another. Kroker points out that "In the simulacrum, reality itself disappears, just vanishes, and what takes its place is a mediascape infected [by] the dynamic logic of the hyper-reality" (*PI* 65). Consider one example of the hyperreal exchange of television for real life, an MTV show called *The Real World*, in which a group of strangers is filmed living together. No longer are real experiences represented; instead, one finds the hyperreality of simulated "real-living." This is the total transparency of simulacra, in which every social moment is always already nothing but simulation. Kroker adds: "Television is the real world of a postmodern culture whose ideology is entertainment ... driven onwards by the universalization [into signs] of the commodity-form" (*PS* 269). Movies such as *Ed-TV* and *The Truman Show* and newly interactive "voyeur television" shows featuring media-manipulated real-life (e.g., the recent incarnation, *Big Brother*) reveal this all too eerily. If the "contestants" lives fail to entertain us (Big Brother?) we simply vote them out. On the *Gilligan's Island* spin-off *Survivor*, real people are made castaways for our viewing pleasure until they're kicked off the island and straight onto TV talk shows and advertisements.

Television and video, in a literal sense, have replaced the real world with a pervasive (and cynical or "cool") image system. As Andre Agassi says, speaking for Canon cameras: "Image is everything" (and simultaneously nothing, as Sprite tells us in its advertisement that deconstructs the other hyperreal commercials out there: "*I believe* that four out of five dentists ... *I believe* that women play basketball in high heeled shoes", etc.). "Image is nothing; obey your thirst." These commercials are hyperreal constructions—created by marketing producers—that parody the postmodern moment, because everyone already knows the electronic medium (the nihilism of an information society) defines the real. A perfect example is the definition of reality provided for us daily by McDonald's. In "McReality," McDonald's advertises the "Real Meal" for kids—as if there were anything "real" to the Big Mac. From prefabbed buns that talk (the "hamburglar") to processed soybean burgers, consumers are given hamburgers as simulacra. The perfect hyperreality exists in "McReality," because McDonald's is the *real* staple food for Americans, from the construction worker or the businessperson who eats there daily, to Mom and the kids on a weekend shopping trip. We know this for certain because we see them on TV. In fact, when what were once referred to as "real" hamburgers are measured against McDonald's burgers as the standard in the commercial ("Mom, it's not the same as McDonald's"), and real moms are measured against McMom's who care enough to bring the kids to McDonald's, we truly have entered the simulacrum: McFamilies in the McReality of an astral McAmerica. And it is no longer geographically limited—Muscovites stand in line for hours in Moscow for a "real taste" of America that is perfectly reproduced, without variance, in every burger.

Where does one come to rest? For Baudrillard: "One's very sense of reality teeters when confronted with an excess of unassimilated (and unassimilable) information, or with a host of hyperreal images which construct the 'reality' of desire" (Singer 141-142). In this scenario, reality comes to us as circulatory prepackaged "desire" created by technocratic means. Singer asserts that:

> One is less entrapped by illusion than absorbed by the simulated models of a reality that would model the apparent reality of our desire. In effect, the collapse of the distinction between appearance and reality ... must be considered the beginning of the end of that perspectival space within which the self situates its relation to others and their limits. If one then pushes the hypothesis further ... one imagines a radically "narcisstic" or "digital" universe where communication becomes ubiquitous and instantaneous, but also empty and circular, and an endless proliferation without external mediation. It is at this point that one begins to perceive the ultimate triumph of a ludic world. (148)

In an advertisement for CDI (interactive computer disks) by Phillips Electronics, the answer to the question of "the meaning of life" is "sold" as interactive (simulated) experience. Like a futuristic *Wizard of Oz* that is already upon us, a man stands in front of the controlling screen, desiring the answer, only to find that it lies before him in electronically mediated form. But what lies behind the curtain/screen to produce his desires? Nothing (but what he makes of it); it is all there on the surface. In postmodern culture there is no return to the real through desire, only a plunge further into the vortex of technological simulation and cyber relations.

At this interface between human and electronic image, in the continuous free-flow circuitry of the cathode ray, production appears as the operative measure of "desire" (as nothing-itself) and subjects are seen as desiring-machines linked to the techno-grid of image-production, sign-production, and consumption-production (*AO* 16). In the world of postmodern communication and information processing, everything is connected, synthesized, mobilized, interrupted, and linked by an economy of desire—not merely desire as lack, but late-capitalist desire as code. The flow of signs as commodities spreads out across the social in simulated form. At this juncture society enters "the hyperspectacle with such intensity that the commodity-form finally breaks free from its grounding in materiality, becoming a sign-form in a circulating machinery of immaterial desires" (*PI* 65). As the commodity form is transformed into a free-floating sign form, where ice-skating polar bears illustrate that Coke is "Always" the "Real Thing," the "lack" (of the cynical sign, of the aphanesthetic subject's desire) can now be (re)produced infinitely, since its image has supplanted the real. Baudrillard stresses "seduction" as opposed to "production" for this very reason: it is (masculine) desire that reproduces itself in commodity form, "a will to power" imposed upon the world as object. Keystone beer advertises "wouldn't it be great if...." and you will the rest (buxom women, island resorts, and inebriation). Not to be outdone, Miller Lite beer gives us Lawyer Rodeos and asks: "Can your beer deliver this?"

In the coding of postmodernity, "desire" exists as a void of empty signs, and proliferate images, and is (re)produced as commodities (simulacra) to be consumed by qualitatively indistinguishable subject-consumers. The fatal objects of identity, the body, and so forth, become simulated, commodified images, and circulated lacks (sign forms). Nietzsche's nihilism ("will to will" or "last will") foretold the fate of late-capitalist consumerist culture all along. The process of postmodernization perpetuates and reifies certain kinds of lived experiences (masculine cultural ideals, and the order of simulation), while "[i]ndividuals who stand outside this preferred reality are doomed to experience alienation, resentment, detachment, strangeness, depersonalization, commodified sexuality, blocked desire, and continual estrangement from the 'objective' worlds of postmodern cultural values" (Denzin 45). Here, at the locus of the object (referentiality) and the empty image (as lived experience): "*production* as the dominant (material) scheme of the industrial order—gives way to *simulation* as the dominant scheme of an order regulated by the 'code' (and thus by the loci of signification)" (*PS* 179). The postmodern "self," all events, and all meanings, are defined and interpreted in terms of this (capitalist/consumerist) code. As Norman K. Denzin puts it, rephrasing Debord: "*lived experience, in terms of its hyperreal representations, has become the final commodity in the circulation of capital*" (44). At karaoke night in your local bar, in the latest ritual of entertainment consumption, you can reproduce yourself on a wide screen TV, becoming part of some B-rated video onto which your image is superimposed, and into which the "DJ" technologically blends your voice. Thus, against the logic of late-capitalist desire as production, and as the challenge of simulation, Baudrillard poses seduction, the surface play of appearance, signs, and image, to unmask the order by which late-capitalism offers to falsely reconcile the image with its unattainable referent (reality, happiness, escape from fears, etc.), and declares further that "Above all, seduction supposes not a signified desire, but the beauty of an artifice" (*SED* 76).

In his article "For a Critique of the Political Economy of the Sign," Baudrillard builds his cultural theory of objects around the idea that the fundamental basis for analyzing "consumptions" is not use value and the relation of needs, but exchange value. The worth of commodity-images (objects, bodies, and information) is affixed more to their value as signs—exchangeable against each other, not against the real—than to their (material) production (*SE&D* 7). In this formulation, value is not the use of the object, but rather, what it can represent (its mediatized form). Now there is superstructure without base. No longer is a "false-consciousness" reified in the historical production and consumption of goods; there is only the circulation of late-capitalist semiurgical code. Baudrillard writes in the "Politcal Economy of the Sign" that reality as we experience it is "'reinterpreted by the sign form, articulated into models and administered by the code (just as the commodity is not what is produced industrially, but what is mediatized by the exchange value system of abstraction)'" (qtd. in Kellner 75). In other words, the exchange of commodities is transformed into a reification and consumption not of the object itself, but of signs. Mike Featherstone writes that "For Adorno the increasing dominance of exchange value not only obliterated the original use-value of things and replaced it by abstract exchange value, but left the commodity free to take on an erstaz or secondary use-value, what Baudrillard was later to refer to as 'sign-value'" (67). Moreover, the predominance of late-capitalist consumer code has resulted in the commodity becoming a sign (85). Most of us are aware that our preferences in clothing, cars, and music are readable as signifiers of taste, personality, and wealth. As such, consumer culture has become a system of sign production whose ubiquitous logic subsumes the entire social order: "Baudrillard theorizes the logic of the sign as the emblematic expression in consumer culture of the commodity-form" (*PS* 179). Commodities that circulate as signs further reproduce the late-capitalist consumer code. Following from the self-referential system of "the code," everything collapses into simulation (*SE&D* 8).

Baudrillard's (ritual) theory of seduction proceeds from a survival ethics against the strategy of the (re)production of culture in commodity (fetishized signs) form. Kroker confirms:

> In the *simulational* scheme of advanced capitalist society, use-value and exchange value conflate into mirrored aspects of a single process of abstract, semiological reproduction: the classical poles of signifier and signified dilate into a single structural homology at the nucleus of the logic of the sign. Baudrillard's challenge is then to strip away the subjectivity of use-value (the referential chain of signifieds) from critical cultural analysis, and examine the purely relational and objective scheme for "free floating" and "semiurgical" objects. (*PS* 180)

In the coding logic of consumer culture, the production of "real" commodity forms with material use values is replaced by the pure sign form—the sign as free-floating commodity (Olalquiaga 19). Today, the order of consumption (late-capitalist code) is nothing but a manipulation of cynical signs and the commodification of empty images, based on a principle of undecidability, neutralization, and indifference (*SE&D* 9). As Gane observes: "Previous contradictions are now neutralized or integrated into a new framework: one in which demand based on new ideology of needs arises on the basis of a new mode of simulation" (111). At this stage of late-capitalism, production of the original gives way to simulation and to the logic of the (cynical) sign as the locus of the real.

In late-capitalism, disinvested subjectivity (that "possessed" by mediascape) moves from a productivist culture to one based on the consumption of signs, in which the symbolic order shifts into simulation. Celeste Olalquiaga writes:

> Free from the restraints of a fixed referentiality, signs can travel openly through the circuits of meaning, ready to be taken up or left arbitrarily, connecting in ways that were previously unthinkable. That signs no longer convey depth but rather remain at surface value speaks of their break with the symbolic, where signification is produced by a strategic positioning within an elaborate and hierarchical system of presence and absence, as in

the concrete representation of abstract meaning. As opposed to such a system, the current constitution of signs occurs through allegorical signification, which highlights the here and now of the sign, reaffirming its most concrete attributes. (21)

If it follows from Jacques Lacan that we desire to define ourselves outside of "the self" in the Symbolic (via signs, in an intralinguistic structure) and as social subjects of ideologies (familial, religious, and political), then the new media social structures have redirected the grid away from ideological (re)production of *desire* toward consumption of signs themselves that function as commodities (identity as simulacrum, lifestyles as images, real world as hologram, etc.). Where else is this more evident than in the *real world* of TV, in which the commodity form operates as a pure image system, and where the mediascape "works as a simulacrum of electronic images recomposing everything into the semiurgical world of advertising and power, which links a processed world based on the exteriorisation of the senses with the interiorisation of simulated *desire* in the form of programmed need-dispositions?" (*PS* 267). In this phase of capitalism, we "define ourselves" in terms of consumption: "Be Young; Drink Pepsi!" Needs are socially generated as part of the signification grid. Consumption is the never-fulfilled desire to perpetually become "signed." (Pepsi begins a "new" campaign before the latest is even launched.)

Western culture has trained us to replace our primary needs with those of becoming "signed" via consumption, so that we feel our needs are being fulfilled when we purchase. Instead of attaining commodities with "use-values," only empty "images" circulate in exchange between the subject and object. The "subject" defines itself in terms of the object's double in the sign/image form—this is the seduction of late-capitalism into image and away from the material. Subjectivity itself becomes the derivative of "decoded" commodity images—a virtual ghost in the capitalist/consumerist machine based on "exchange" (Massumi 201). For Baudrillard: "Consumer behaviour, which appears to be focused and directed at the object and at pleasure, in fact responds to quite different objectives: the metaphoric or displaced expression of desire, and the production of a code of social values through the use of differentiating signs" (*SW* 46). The code has taught us to identify with what lies on the surface of the object consumed (such qualities as "natural," "better," "tradition," "stronger," "America," "family values," and "cleanliness"). The individual is bombarded with such advertising, making it seem that products fulfill the desire to "belong," to be "secure"—providing us with simulated identity in the empty form of electronic blips on a screen. An obscene consumption of surface and electronic images circulates as the reality that fills the void of nihilism. Television exists as a triumph of the postmodern "filler," creating out of the void a very real world of electronic images, cultural signification, identity holograms, and lifestyle illusions.

Hyperreal America is a feeding ground for virtual/cynical consumption where the postmodern subject consumes images of consumption and codes of desire, the simulacra of postmodern culture. Individuals are now programmed to (re)produce and consume simulacra: (re)presentation of the "lack" (desire) has replaced the material "object" of desire with the "objective" of consumption. This fatal strategy is facilitated by the screenal circulation of consumer codes by the media and by the constant reprocessing of "desire" into images. Desire is the hologram of late capitalism—the empty "images" serve as commodities for the postmodern individual who daily experiences the externalization of the body at the television screen, and the colonization of the real by the image. As the commodity (dis)appears into the expanse of its own simulacrum (how many different brands of corn flakes can one buy that are "really" the same?), individuals consume the signs of consumption, where the image represents nothing other than consumption itself. In this self-serving industry: "The commodity has become a form of capital with its own motor of exchange (fashion, style, 'self-improvement') and cycle of realization (image accumulation/image shedding. . . ." (Massumi 200). This is what Kroker terms "capital accumulation which is, anyway, entering its last, purely aesthetic phase: the phase of designer bodies, designer environments, and simulation models as signs of the Real" (*PS* 18). Hyperaesthetics—as the production and consumption of the simulacra—is no more evident than the fashion, advertising, and media industries from which, as Barbara Kruger says: "we buy in order to be."

Hence we return again to Nietzsche's "will," the human necessity to create out of nothingness. Only now, when the Gulf War (which "occurred" as a made-for-TV miniseries), *Code 3*, and the O. J. Simpson trial (covered from "gavel to gavel" on E!) become hyperreal forms of entertainment, one is forced to admit that the real no longer exists, that it only appears to us "as a vast and seductive simulation" (*PS* 186). How else might you explain the fact that the TV cameras awaited the invasion of Somalia, as if on some sort of Hollywood movie set? The hyperaesthetics experienced comes straight from the fatal strategies of the will to power, of the creator (*der Schaffende*), of a promotional culture in which the commodity form of late capitalism becomes image in the (empty) rhetoric of "recommodification." Kroker asserts that "the perfect nihilists would always prefer to will cynically than not to will at all. Baudrillard's world of the *simulacrum* is the perfect freedom of remaking [redoubling] the world in a universe which provides no purpose to our willing . . . he has discovered the 'pure sign' to be the essence and secret destiny of the commodity form"(*PS* 186). Nietzsche's legacy of the "last man" is now obvious. While we "will to will" as a condition of existence in the nihilistic cycle of consuming the signs of consumption provided by a recombinant culture: "Nietzsche's 'pessimism' (which is really the method of 'perspectival' understanding) becomes an entirely *realistic* strategy for exploring postmodern experience. And this event, the interpretation of advanced capitalist society under the sign of nihilism is the basic condition for human emancipation as well as for the recovery of the tragic sense of critical theory" (*PS* 187).

Chapter Four

Technology and the (Dis)appearing Subject: Schizophrenia or Seduction?

> The obscenity of our culture resides in the confusion of desire and its equivalent materialized in the image; not only for sexual desire, but in the desire for knowledge and its equivalent materialized in "information."
>
> —Jean Baudrillard, *The Ecstasy of Communication*

> Everywhere today, after centuries of triumphant subjectivity, the irony of the object lies in wait for us, an objective irony readable at the very heart of information and of science, at the very heart of the system and its laws, at the heart of desire and of all psychology.
>
> —Jean Baudrillard, *Fatal Strategies*

Within the interstices of the circuitry of the electronic code, the binary signal of the one and zero, the replication of the DNA model, or the links of voice mail, Jean Baudrillard meets Giles Deleuze and Felix Guattari. Here one finds the (dis)appearing subject and the circulating codes of *desire*. In technoculture, the subject's desire enters into simulation. Functioning in a "horizontalized" world of perspectival appearances, the "self" exists as a topology of the purely cynical sign. Here, the subject finds itself as the hyperaestheticized (image-saturated) object—"where living means simulation" (*PI* 2). There is increasingly little difference between our reality and what is depicted daily on television in "real world" TV shows, in live coverage of wars and natural catastrophes, and in the advertising industry's conversion of public and private space into terminal networks through which desire is created by image saturation, later reified in the consumption process (thus becoming "real"). One can hardly escape participation in the virtual world of mediascape, consumerism, fashion, art, and so forth. The postmodern subject that can only "will" a world to replace its lack occupies a purely virtual and relational space of images. Calling on Friedrich Nietzsche, Kroker describes the postmodern experience as "subjectivity to a point of aesthetic excess that the self no longer has any real existence, only a perspectival appearance as a site where all the referents converge and implode" (*PI* 5). Techno-culture is no longer the world as representation, in which the vestiges of perspectival space remain distinct, but a simulated world coming at us: "a 'semio-aesthetics' in which the 'objects' of technology are 'projected' towards the eye as its own internal vanishing point" (*PI* 77). In this scenario, the individual becomes the object of cultural imagery. Such parasitic violence feeds off a "nearly instantaneous 'possession' of 'our' bodies by an ultramodern mechanics of inFORMation" (Pfohl 256). Stephen Pfohl writes:

> [A] major transformation in the sacrificial constitution of human subjectivity has been taking place. This, moreover, is occurring with such power that (blank white) masses of people may be no longer so much repressed as expressed (or ecstatically empowered) as they are transferentially waved between screens of inFORMation and parasitically mounted by increasingly automated sign-systems. In this, waves of inFORMational power may pass into and envelop our bodily imaginations like simulated or premodeled tele-electronic *loa* that ride us, their human-animal-machine hosts from one end of the globe to the other. (256)

For example, the TV screen ritually "informs" individuals of who they are, what makes them happy, what they fear and desire; they need merely stay "Plugged In" to MTV. So many of us are lured by the prospects of the perfect body or the perfect existence—all prefigured in a perfect simulacrum, our doubling within the circulatory and free-floating media scene.

In the individual possessed by the "cybernetic-capital" of technological society, one finds Nietzsche's "apparent self" operating in "the space of an accidental topology and seductive contiguity of aesthetic effects" (*PI* 5). At this point, production and consumption give way to the promiscuity of the network: a "narcissistic and protean era of connections, contact, contiguity, feedback, and generalized interface that goes with the universe of communication" (Baudrillard, *The Anti-Aesthetic* 127). Here, one locates a cybernetic space of postmodern subjectivity based on the negative-feedback of premodeled simulations of individuality (Pfohl 257). According to Kroker, this describes the "evolution of technological nihilism up to its stage of simulation, and, thereupon to the age of sacrificial [doubling] culture" (*PI* 19) where individuals are presented with "the contemporary human situation of living at the violent edge of primitivism and simulation, of indefinite reversibility in the order of things wherein only the excessive cancellation of difference through violence re-energizes the process" (*PI* 18-19). This is a call to the techno-culture that finally puts to rest the rationalist eschatology that Nietzsche so resented. Ours is a "virtual" world so saturated by technological images that the fantasy of the real is once and for all ended. In the simulacra of the techno-culture, hyperreality comes to life, and the image is materialized: "an image-reservoir of subjectivity that we insist on calling material reality" (*PS* 79). Here Nietzsche's "will to will" comes to full light in technology, and the logic of seduction may be embraced, for all of us are willing victims in the process. It is the nihilistic struggle of existence in which life is exchanged for semiological being: "Not really a human world, but a hyper-human one: that point where subjectivity inscribes itself in the commodity first, then in the sign, and finally in the sacrificial violence immanent to seduction" (*PI* 80). Into this horizontal cyberflow of a purely relational sign, the topological play of appearances, and the technological processing or doubling of images, travels the postmodern subject. This is a pure entry into the spiraling abyss of language (Lacan), into the telemetried body (Critical Art Ensemble), the ecstasy of pure communication and circulation of code (Baudrillard), or nomadic lines of flight from the production of desire (Deleuze and Guattari). There, it encounters what Kroker calls "the enchanted world of technological eschatology . . . the trompe l'oeil [as the illusion of the real] comes alive, [where] everything wants desperately to escape the terrorism of the referent, and enter into the surface play of appearances" (*PI* 78).

Moving finally through Baudrillard's critique of rationalism, past the shift of the commodity form to the sign form, what results is an eschatology of technological culture in which everything material finally disappears at the site of its digital double; that is, technology, as an illusion of the real, itself becomes the world (*SW* 44). According to Kroker, technology is an object of fascination only when it is about

> the disappearance of commodities into signs, history into simulation, material objects into image reservoirs, faces with memories into the surgical world of designer aesthetics, bodies into fractal subjectivity, the spoken word into communication, and panoptic space into the enchanted simulacrum of the trompe l'oeil. And all this world of disappearances, not as the false consciousness of a real antecedent world, but as the brilliant destiny, the point of immanent reversibility, towards which the language of seduction lures us, and for the sake of which it struggles to survive. (*PI* 78)

In a darkening universe, Baudrillard ultimately turns to technology as seduction—no longer an age of simulacra, but of holographic logic as the ecstatic moment of the sign's fatal fulfillment. We find ourselves already entering at hyperspeed a world of digital seduction, the world of the mediascape and the smooth surface of communication (*PI* 64). The seduction of techno-culture is its ability to turn material reality into a world of semio-aesthetics. In this process, where the sign replaces the real, the exchange is one of abstract, "hypersymbolic" diffusions of information—a maximum production of words/meanings/images in which historical subjects are constituted as simulacra, so that what used to be perceived as metaphor is projected into reality "entirely without metaphor, into an absolute space of simulation" (*EC* 16). That is, we are no longer Nietzschean characters self-creating on stage—the networks now choreograph it all for us. Here, at the "code made flesh," to be human means to exist as a fractal subject in the language of advertising—a hyperaestheticized world of information processing and virtual imagery that lacerates the body and inscribes its logic on the flesh. In *The Ecstasy of Communication*, Baudrillard posits: "In the image of television . . . the surrounding universe and our very bodies are becoming monitoring screens" (*EC* 12). Just watch MTV's video by Porno for Pyros, in which fractal bodies dance and sing across the screen in a continuous flow—the final ecstatic realization of the world as an image reservoir that "always runs on empty" (*PI* 79).

The completion of Baudrillard's thought move us from hyperreality into a totally cybernetic space, where the fate of subjectivity resembles that found in the digital world of *Lawnmower Man*, where virtual reality is like an irresistible pathology (addiction) that infects us. Kroker states:

> [I]f McLuhan could think of technology as disease, it was anticipatory of Baudrillard's later reflections on the cold universe of digital technology as a form of viral contamination, or *evil*, that takes possession of subjectivity, making of it the site of a fantastic proliferation of cynical signs, like a cancer cell. Here, the exteriorization of the central nervous system in the mediascape which McLuhan predicted finds its moment of historical completion in Baudrillard's theorization of hyper-reality. (*PI* 69)

It appears to be our human destiny to become the terminals on which the hyperreality of information plays itself out in a world of mass communication and its seductions. In this era of "private telematics," many of us find our/selves "at the controls of a hypothetical machine, isolated in a position of perfect and remote sovereignty" (*EC* 15). Garnered from the virtual power of telematics, television and computer screens now serve as the orbital universe of the individual. We somehow find ourselves already having entered the cyberuniverse that William Gibson's *Neuromancer* describes so vividly for us. No longer are we relegated to the confines of our work or our domestic and community environments: "Today, it is the very space of habitation that is conceived as both receiver and distributor, as the space of reception and operations, the control screen and terminal which as such may be endowed with telematic power—that is, with the capability of regulating everything from a distance, including work in the home, and of course consumption, play, social relations, and leisure" (*AA* 128). Look, for example, at phone sex (1-900's—teledildonics is to follow), which has now entered the era of computer bulletin board "orgies," video games, Sunday NFL Football, virtual teleconferences, and modems to communicate with the office. It is no longer necessary to engage in these activities physically (i.e., go to the ballpark, or even report to work)—they are all accessible through the terminal. Through the promiscuity of the network, you can be anyone or anywhere you want to be; just click on your mouse. The flip side to this miniaturization of time and space is that the real loses out to the screenal, suddenly appearing as cumbersome and useless (*EC* 18). The value of all real experience disappears into its event scene double on the screen; this includes personal relationships and romance (from soap operas, to personal tragedies, to social events such as the ball game or the cinema)—all disappear into terminally accessible screenal experiences in the commodity form of entertainment. The social event itself has become a mediatized and commercialized giant space of circulation. In an obscene gesture, private and public space merge before us on the screen. Baudrillard points out: "Obscenity begins when there is no more spectacle, no more stage, no more illusion, when everything becomes immediately transparent, visible, exposed in the raw and inexorable light of information and communication" (*EC* 21-22).

The interaction of the electronic mass media with "the social" brings about an implosion of meaning (as delusion) and an explosion of information (as real). Baudrillard's essay "The Implosion of Meaning in the Media" operates under one main thesis—that more and more information produces less and less meaning (*In the Shadow of the Silent Majorities* 95). The information processing of the history, reality, and subjectivity of electronic mass media nullifies signification: "we are gorged with meaning and it is killing us" (*EC* 63). Information processing as the fatal destiny of the cynical sign transforms itself into the "ecstasy of communication." Baudrillard describes the effects of the technological society: "Ecstasy is all functions abolished into one dimension, the dimension of communication. All events, all spaces, all memories are abolished in the sole dimension of information: this is obscene" (*EC* 23-24). In postmodern society, the spectacle is abolished, and the obscenity of information networks and communication circuitry reigns (*EC* 22). The media are obscene in their crusade to detail every event, a process of communication that so often makes the object or the referent disappear (*FS* 88) into an ecstasy of the circulating "will"—into the inner curvatures of the viewer's eye/"I"(Pfohl 72).

With the disappearance of the scene and the development of mass communication and the media, a new form of subjectivity emerges in which individuals become saturated with the ecstatic form of the real: information, images, and simulations. Without distance, they become pure screens, or switching centers for the influent networks, circuits, simulation models, systems of recording and all surfaces of inscription (*FS* 85). It is both dangerous and pathological—a schizophrenic vertigo that seeks to make all reality purely transparent, exact, and immaterial. Like the recent telecommunications commercial: "There will be no there, only here." The schizophrenic's astral eye/"I" cannot escape the immediacy of a transparent world-as-sign that serves as the very sight of its disappearance. Baudrillard warns of the schizophrenic:

> [not] characterized by his loss of touch with reality, but by the absolute proximity to and total instantaneousness with things, this overexposure to the transparency of the world. Stripped of a stage and crossed over without the least obstacle, the schizophrenic cannot produce the limits of his very being, he can no longer produce himself as a mirror. He becomes a pure screen, a pure absorption and resorption surface of the influent networks. (*EC* 27)

As the individual becomes part of these immanent communication networks, the subject is diffused across electronic space, into both infinite space and instantaneous oscillation as subject and object. Both "being" and "becoming" are instantly transposed, simultaneously here and elsewhere—on the screen, the virtual body spreads across the network, selves materialize as the many, and evaporate into empty (cyber)space.

Within the nihilism that marks techno-culture, the subject disappears into pure simulated space, what Celeste Olalquiga calls a "psychasthenic dissolution" into the surrounding world (17). At this hi-tech schizophrenic juncture, being and surroundings fuse into one, and bodies fragment and disappear (1). Olalquiga asserts: "Technology is gradually displacing the organic in favor of the cybernetic and the symbolic with the imaginary, producing a fragmentation of "the self" that is compensated in the intensification of pornographic and painful pleasure" (1). Identity, in this ecstatic form, operates as a purely virtual and relational space of images (*PI* 5). Identity as simulacrum is now free-floating desire, ready to attach to any sign-commodity form. This is evidenced, for instance, in Busch beer commercials where "to be a mountain man you don't even have to be a Man." TV culture, then, is a "perfect description, in short, of the *virtual body*, of the *virtual self*: the self that has no real corporeal existence, only an affective existence as a temporary, always mobile, almost mathematical, site for the remapping of experience. . . . Not corporeality but the 'body without organs,' not Being but becoming, not Species, but 'machinic assemblies'" (*PI* 115). For Baudrillard, both the body and "the self" (is there a difference in a hyperreality where both must conform to images?) can be divided and commodified, as governed by the capitalist/advertising code. To see the "self" as a technology possessed by the mediascape, as Baudrillard does, is to become schizophrenic.

As identity merges into the electronic image, the schizoanalysis of Deleuze and Guattari may offer a less pessimistic way of understanding the condition of the postmodern subject than Baudrillard's concession to the commodity fetishism and to the abstraction of the code. The schizophrenic can produce any flow, any coupling of pure desire. The "flow" (information, technology, and images) is the realm of the schizo who "consumes all of universal history in one fell swoop" (*AO* 21). This happens all the time on television, from Charlie Chaplin selling computers to the latest documentary. As Kroker explains: "TV is *information society* to the hyper, just though where information means the liquidation of the social, the exterminism of memory (in the sense of human remembrance as aesthetic judgment), and the substitution of the simulacrum of a deterretorialized and dehistoricized image-system for actual historical contexts" (*PS* 275). The schizoid identifies the territories of history with BwO (body without organs as diffused states of potential "becomings") like a "Nietzschean subject who passes through a series of states, and who identifies these states with the names of history: '*every name in history is I*'" (*AO* 21). In the process, the schizoid subject deterritorializes and reterritorializes meanings across the BwO as an expression of individual desire. The body without organs "can be thought of as the constellation of part-objects governing a given body's tendencies in becoming, or its desires" (Massumi 184). As both product and producer in techno-culture, the schizoid is the diffused "subject who spreads itself out along the entire circumference of the circle, the center of which has been abandoned by the ego. At the center is the desiring machine" (*AO* 21).

For Deleuze and Guattari, "desire" is produced in the entire machinery of the body without organs (*TP* 149). The BwO is a "connection of desires, conjunction of flows, continuum of intensities" (*TP* 161). Desire is flow and interruption between the molar and the molecular, the aggregate of the wave and particle, the cohesive force of the rhizomatic existence of "becoming" (*TP* 21). Deleuze and Guattari write in *Anti-Oedipus* that "In desiring-machines everything functions at the same time, but amid hiatuses and ruptures, breakdowns and failures, stallings and short circuits, distances and fragmentation . . . desiring-production is pure multiplicity, that is to say, an affirmation that is irreducible to any sort of unity" (42). Hence, Deleuze and Guattari confirm the production and consumption of desires as a "becoming," a nomadic line of flight through which the (fractal) subject may proceed to exist in the hyperaesthetic and hyperhistorical (hysterical?) overcoding of our postmodern world. This type of "nomadic" thought "does not repose on identity; it rides difference" (Massumi 5).

In contrast to Baudrillard, who would pursue desire into the detritus of its own simulacrum, Deleuze and Guattari proclaim the need to reaffirm desire-as-production. The "schiz"—as uncoded flows of desire—"serves as a point of departure as well as a point of destination" (*AO* xix). The "schizzes," the breaks, the aporias that breed heterogeneity are vital interstices that connect and conduct the whole. The "whole" assemblage here is to be seen as a limit that is never achievable, except in collectivity as an aggregate. For Deleuze and Guattari: "The schizoanalytic argument is simple: desire is a machine, a synthesis of machines, a mechanic arrangement—desiring-machines. The order of desire is the order of *production*; all production is at once desiring-production and social production" (*AO* 296). Deleuze and Guattari reproach the institution of psychoanalysis for "stifling this order of production, for having shunted it into *representation*" (*AO* 296). They call for a collective subjectivity to heal the sickness of humanity (Oedipalization) (*AO* xxi). All philosophy has colluded in creating an artificial division between the "domains of representation, subject, concept, and being" that Deleuze and Guattari wish to "replace with a conductivity that knows no bounds" (Massumi 5).

As the great referents ("Truth," "Beauty," "Reality," "the Self," "the Social," etc.) disperse into an entirely nihilistic and electronic order of signs, the schizophrenic machine becomes the perfect metaphor. The schizoid subject is the pure screen for a digitally programmed flow of codes. The human, as desiring machine, fragments into a "chasm" of cynical, paranoiac signs (economic, psychological, moral, political, and ideological). Individuals locate the foci of machines where the circulation of the signs of desire in simulacra are all that matter—the ceaseless transformation of codes (rhizomatic deterritorialization) along the techno-grid. The consuming machine traverses the terrain of (de)coded flows, dematerialized bodies (BwO), and (de)contextualized desire into a realm of signs without signifieds. In this schizo equation, the representational consumerist technology crashes at a "virtual" sight (i.e., *the circulation of simulated/dead capital and empty/cynical power meet the screen*).[1] In its midst Nietzsche again surfaces: Is this the "becoming-human?"

At the crossroads of Baudrillard and Deleuze and Guattari, where the individual is possessed with a virtual mediascape, everything again returns to Nietzsche. But this return finally leaves us with two ways of reading through his thought. First, there is the dark and fatal side of Nietzsche that is processed through Baudrillard. In Baudrillard's writing, one confronts nihilism at its fully aestheticized stage: "technology as a theater of seduction" (*PI* 72). His contemporary strategy of seduction "would counter the surveillance and computer processes, the ever more sophisticated methods of biological and molecular control and retrieval of bodies, all the procedures of identification" (*EC* 74-75). Secondly, there is the "rhizomatic" side of affirmation and "becoming" found in Deleuze and Guattari. While Baudrillard wearily invites a future in which meaning and "difference" flatten in technological proliferation (all possibilities are recognized), Deleuze and Guattari shift to new forms of signification through multiple associations at different semiotic levels, strata, and plateaus—such as hypertext writing or Critical Art Ensemble's multimedia performances.

Like Nietzsche, Deleuze and Guattari's rhizomatic philosophy stresses "becoming" against "being" as a potential transformative state for existence. Kroker insists that Deleuze and Guattari describe "the hyper-modern individual: trapped within the heavy gravity of a body with organs, drained of its creative energies by the demands of historicized subjectivity; but always with the possibility of becoming" (*PI* 116). Deleuze and Guattari call for no less than push[ing] the simulacra to a point where they cease being artificial images to become indices of the new world. That is what the completion of the process is: not a promised and a pre-existing land, but a world created in the process of its tendency, its coming undone, its deterretorialization... and produce the new land—not at all a hope, but a simple "finding," a "finished design," where the person who escapes causes other escapes, and marks out the land while deterretorializing himself. (*AO* 322)

Deleuze and Guattari exalt the rhizomatic deterritorialization of the schizophrenic process. Yet Baudrillard argues for seduction against the rhizomatic production and recuperation of difference through "becoming." Kroker writes:

> Baudrillard focuses on the disappearing cultural space of the real and the counterfeit, only to project its violent implosion into simulation, thereupon into fractal subjectivity. Against the order of simulation, [Deleuze and Guattari] want to recover the possibility of the rematerialization of experience: a rhizomatic network of experience where events vanish into a decoded world of immateriality, only to instantly reappear in their opposite sign form in an endless chain of "lines" of flight and interruption. (*PI* 120)

A rhizome deterritorializes desiring assemblages through complex molecular lines of flight (*TP* 506), like proliferate roots spreading in multiple directions, that connect (m)any points on (m)any planes. The rhizome is made up like lines on a map, not points—just expansion, connection, heterogeneity, and multiplicity. Any point on a rhizome can and must be connected to others. There is no subject/object relationship, and there is the principle of a-signifying rupture. Oversignifying may rupture across the structure, but a rhizome will submerge and reemerge to proceed again on new lines.

Like Nietzsche, this sort of thinking stresses "becoming" against edifying; renewal and life against ideation and being; and desire and will against representation and simulacrum. Multiplicities of the rhizome type are always in the middle, always operating across a plane of "becoming," a body without organs, never total, never final (*TP* 507). In this collective process, existence is made up of anthropomorphic as well as anorganic strata comprising life: "becoming-human," "becoming-animal," and "becoming-stone." Everything connects in molecular lines, through heterogeneous plateaus. One never reaches "becoming"; "becoming" is always middle (*TP* 503). The schizophrenic recognizes the multiplicities of *becoming* along the rhizomatic grid: the multiplicity of deterritoriality and reterritoriality, the experience of belonging to smooth space that transforms "the self" and the one into the many, the composite (*TP* 505). The schizophrenic embodies the free association of animal-vegetable-mineral, an infinitely changing sign, a will to power without limits. That is why the body without organs and the schizophrenic represent the perfect sign slide, the subject disappearing into a regime of cynical signs. The BwO is a continuum of the decoded relations, desires, and flows across which the organism, signification, and subjectivity are composed (*TP* 159-161).

Deleuze and Guattari's *A Thousand Plateaus* gives the formulation of schizo living, of the BwO, and of lines of flight for a "subjectivity in ruins" (*PI* 55). They assert: "In its destructive task, schizoanalysis must proceed as quickly as possible, but it can also only proceed by successively undoing the representative territorialities and reterritorializations through which a subject passes in his individual history" (*AO* 318). What Deleuze and Guattari propose in "rhizomatics" or "schizonalysis" is a logic that is not "between things" but perpendicular, passing through planes, composing by the logic of the "and," which nullifies beginnings and endings (*TP* 25). Rooted in this path, one again senses the presence of Nietzsche who calls for active forgetting (deterritorializing) and creating new territories over remembering or tracing old ones, nomadic dances across plateaus—all matters of metamorphosis and *becomings*. In a truly Nietzschean climate, Deleuze and Guattari write: "A schizoanalysis schizophrenizes in order to break the holds of power and institute research into a new collective subjectivity and revolutionary healing of mankind. For we are sick, so sick of our *selves*!" (*AO* xxi).

The first task of schizoanalysis is to discover in the subject the nature and functioning of his desiring machine so as to de-Oedipalize it, and cleanse it of the virus that teaches us to will our own repression. Schizoanalysis seeks to discover deterritorialized codes that escape the Oedipal coding and allow the subject lines of flight into the BwO and the schizophrenic processing of reality (*AO* xvii). At its heart is a desire to escape the repression of the herd mentality, as expressed by Nietzsche, or as Baudrillard puts it, the masses (the silent majority). "The self" must be seen as part of a continuum of forces always in the process of desiring and production, in all processes of *becomings*. Desire produces life; in recuperating that desire, we produce a reality, as opposed to the will of cynical power (the state apparatuses and the order of simulation). Existence is the flow of energies, and life the flow of desires between objects. As Deleuze and Guattari believe: "every 'object' presupposes the continuity of a flow; every flow the fragmentation of the object. Doubtless each organ-machine interprets the entire world from the perspective of its own flux, from the point of view of the energy that flows from it: the eye interprets everything ... But a connection with another machine is always established" (*AO* 6). Here one finds nothing less than the will to power of the "perspectival," postmodern, nihilistic, technocratic subject. It is, as Deleuze and Guattari remark, the world of the molecular, where flows or lines of flight are always only the pure nothingness of the BwO by which a reality is produced. They point to Artaud who sought to create a form of theater that rediscovered primal gestures, screams, and other stimuli in order to break through the threshold of language to genuine lived experiences, or quantum physics, for that matter, to confirm that this world of microbes is "nothing more than coagulated nothingness"

(*AO* 281). It is our production of desire that creates—out of the molecular nothingness—the social and the real of the molar.

Liberating the schizoid flows across the molar in the postmodern world of hyperaesthetics (surface) and simulacra is one way to combat the inherent nihilism—make anything of it you wish, because multiplicity and alterity are the operative codes. Seize the power in a ludic universe. The schizophrenic's world always flows from the "I," the will of the actively producing "self." The schizophrenic embodies the free association of "becoming animal-vegetable-mineral," with identity as an infinitely sliding sign—a will to power without limits. Kroker holds that the "theology of becoming" at the heart of Deleuze and Guattari's rhizomatic metaphor is nothing less than "the form that nihilism assumes in the age of virtual technology" (*PI* 116). Reading nihilism through the rhizomatic metaphor may open postmodern experience to a new possibility for *becomings*. Kroker acknowledges this: "If later in *A Thousand Plateaus*, they could trace out a more subterranean tradition of 'rhizomatic' resistance, from Spinoza to Artaud and Blanchot, it is only because they seek to materialize the dark, often unread, side of *The Will to Power:* that 'dancing' side where Nietzsche anticipates Heidegger by speaking of 'becoming' as the horizon of recuperated life" (*PI* 110). But, all in all, Kroker argues, Deleuze and Guattari still support the fiction of a "subject" and a "will" able to project a world that is reassuring ("romantic" Marxism). Exactly what Deleuze and Guattari see as the answer may be merely subsumed within its doubling in late-capitalism and the production of simulacra—images of desire, reproduced and circulated electronically as nothing in themselves, merely to parade as the real. If postmodern desire is nothing but a massive poststructural sign-slide, then desire itself becomes simulation (*SED* 5). Nietzsche knew this all along as the sacrificial nihilism intrinsic to the "will to power"—"the fatal sign-slide at the disappearing centre of things" (*PI* 113). Deleuze and Guattari's writing (its doubling) tries to rematerialize the "real" that Nietzsche and Baudrillard knew never existed (except as seduced). Pfohl believes that individuals must ritually enact such representational doublings to "solidly differentiate" them/selves ("subjects-in-flux") from the objects perceived: "Otherwise 'we' humans would remain adrift within the ecstatic but never stable waves of heterogeneous multiplicity, a continuous process of flowing into and out of ever-shifting forms of association" (140). Nietzsche knew this necessary doubling of nothing, at the heart of all existence, as the nihilistic will. As Nietzsche said in *The Genealogy of Morals:* "rather than want nothing, man even wants nothingness" (454).

Whereas Nietzsche tended to affirm nihilism via the will, Baudrillard's position is much more skeptical: meaning is now something to be "played with" in an eternally recurring simulacrum. In this order, Baudrillard adds: "each of the game's sequences delivers us from the linearity of life" (*SED* 146). The "challenge" of postmodernity is no longer one of will, desire, or meaning, but of seduction. Baudrillard contends: "If desire is a will to power and possession, seduction places before it an equal will to power by the simulacrum. In forming a web of appearances, seduction both sustains this hypothetical power of desire and exorcises it" (*SED* 87). This is a universe beyond desire and beyond cynical signs, which, for seduction, only existed in the mythical world of representations and the production of meaning. Now, there is only the challenge of the game, with ritual signs to "deliver us from meaning" (*SED* 137). Baudrillard's games should not be confused with the indeterminacy of "becoming" or with the proliferation of meaning in rhizomatic form that seeks to escape meaning in lines of flight. He suggests in the following passage, that "One does not escape meaning by dissociation, disconnection or deterritorialization. One escapes meaning by replacing it with a more radical simulacrum, a still more conventional order—like the alphabetical order for Barthes, or the rules of a game, or the innumerable rituals of everyday life which frustrate both the (political, historical or social) order of meaning and the disorder (chance) which one would impose on them" (*SED* 138). Baudrillard's "game" theory thus ultimately returns to Nietzsche's idea of the "eternal return"—willed as such. It is a will to seduction that is both tragic and ritual. Ultimately, says Kellner: "Baudrillard interprets seduction as an elaborate ritual or game which breaks with the logic of both production and desire, and which pursues its own aesthetic play on the levels of appearance, signs and fascination" (147).

Chapter Five

Dehistoricized Subjectivity: Reese Williams and the Schizoid Text

Can one consciously act to forget and lose all knowledge?
—Reese Williams, *A Pair of Eyes*

Amid the fatality that marks postmodernism, it seems that "disappearance" is a prevailing undercurrent, chiefly felt in the death of a centered subject (à la Lacan) and the disappearance of its sense of history (Jameson 125). From what Julia Kristeva terms formidable attempts to *"expand the limits of the signifiable,"* (137) twentieth-century Western culture has propagated a bombardment of signification by which to identify and define it/self. The result of this accelerated image processing is a "denigration of meaning (events, history, memory, etc.)" associated with their use (*EDOI* 23). The conscious "experience of limits" has served to desensitize the "reading" subject and erase history's own significance—that is, to create an ahistorical present. In "Postmodernism and Consumer Society," Fredric Jameson claims that "our entire contemporary social system has little by little begun to lose the capacity to retain its own past, has begun to live in a perpetual present and in a perpetual change that obliterates traditions of the kind which all earlier social formations have had in one way or another to preserve" (125). This motion is epitomized by the advertising industry, which has no sense of history, only the hypertrophic production of meaning and a proliferation of reprocessed images. History has literally disappeared into the absolute proximity of its own simulacra: Civil War battles are refought in perfect simulation; Fred Astaire dances (in authentic black and white) with Paula Abdul in Pepsi ads; the deaths of Elvis, Marilyn, and Kennedy remain irreal, wrapped in infinite layers of theories, studies, and media depictions. The hyperreality created is evidenced in the surge of pastiche resulting from nostalgia for a history that somehow seems to have been "lost"—ironically, through its continual presence. Hypertextualization, the montage of self-referential signification that has hastily developed during the latter twentieth century, has brought the regime of the sign (and the postmodern subject) to an ahistorical pass, into the often-silenced, always multiple spaces of cultural schizophrenia. Just "plug-in" for a few moments and experience the effect of MTV, where a continuous flow of diverse and anachronistic images makes them hard to connect in a signifying chain.

Postmodernism, in general, attempts to perceive this "space" where the historical subject "crosses over" into the space of the schizoid Other (Jardine 86). This action becomes a hyperextension, as Alice Jardine puts it, into a "superconsciousness," one without "Images, without Father and without the Mother, without Man or History" (87). This is often the experience of the schizophrenic, who fails to fully enter the symbolic realm of language (Jameson 118). As Jardine warns: "To give new language to these other spaces is a project filled with both promise and fear" (73). For this project necessitates that we recuperate Michel Foucault's first epoch—history's unconscious—"where words were not yet separated from things" (Jardine 84), when being and meaning were synonymous and omnipresent.
[1] The present situation seems to drive us to pass beyond this "zero-point" of language and meaning. This recovery requires, in fact, traversing the space of primitive language, where now only the silence of Madness speaks in an ahistorical and presymbolic system of meaning, where writing designates nothing other than itself (*OT* 304). The postmodern critic, Mike Featherstone, questions whether MTV might not move beyond a Saussurian system of language based on differences, to a new one based on image hyperprocessing (69). This is precisely the journey readers are invited to take upon opening Reese Williams's *A Pair of Eyes*—a schizophrenic text that dehistoricizes and silences the speaking sign, driving it finally into the regress of images and detritus of its own simulacrum.

For the schizophrenic, temporal and spatial continuities break down, and the illusory presence of the world (as signs) becomes "overwhelmingly vivid" (Jameson 120). Postmodern (late-capitalist) culture pushes the sign into an analogous cultural schizophrenia—into a hyperreality where the distinction between reality and representation collapses and breaks the connection to (His)tory that materially oppresses the subject via the dominance of the sign. In this logocentric phenomenon, meaning is derived from the interrelationships of material signifiers—written or uttered words or images—and their signifieds—concepts evoked from the text. From a poststructural viewpoint, it is important to note that writing or sounds are merely arbitrary, yet material, events or things, which by themselves "hold" no meaning. Any temporal moment of meaning is derived via a system of differences that comprise the linguistic "structure" of language and creates reality. Derrida would argue that the meaning of any signified is perpetually deferred away from, or outside of itself; thus the presence of meaning is illusory anyhow. Still, Western culture is "centered" on the illusion of the metaphysics of presence in the signified—a presence that Foucault says disappeared during the first epoch. In the postmodern world this illusion collapses, or "breaks down," in the same way as language does for the schizophrenic.

A Pair of Eyes repeatedly "descends into this grand illusion" to disrupt and disconnect the reader-subject from the historically and ideologically coded regime of the sign, pushing her (as participant in the text) into the realm of the schizophrenic experience. The decentered text of schizoid discourse (free of consumptive "desires") undoes cultural and social markers that have been inscribed on the individual, enabling her to enter the space of free, nomadic subjectivity. Here, one finds the moment of pure materiality, where (as for the schizophrenic) signifiers lose their signifieds and become nothing other than images (Jameson 120), instead of being reified as commodities. Jean Baudrillard refers to this fatal postmodern condition of the signifier as an exponential enfolding of images and messages without end or destination (*EDOI* 30), where the medium (advertising code, or media information) truly is the message. At this point, the subject enters into the pure circulation of late-capitalist code, becoming a metonymic site for the indifferent exchange of signifiers. In this scenario, the individual will be left either in silence/madness (Baudrillard's call for a totally ludic universe), or with the creation of new plateaus, new discursive structures, and territories through which the disinvested subject might drift (interpret, read, and speak) in the Deleuzian sense.

In a schizophrenic system of signification (a schizoid text), the subject or cogito, is itself a floating signifier, floating amid other signifiers. As a searching subject-self, the schizophrenic becomes both subject and object of its own desire—indistinguishable both Self and Other—both signified and signifier at once. Due to the atemporal nature of the schizophrenic experience, she "does not know personal identity in our sense, since our feeling of identity depends on our sense of the persistence of the 'I' and the 'me' over time" (Jameson 119). At this point, perspectival space between subject and object collapses, where free circulation is the operative metaphor. This reflexivity liberates the significance of the "self" from the sociolinguistic structure and creates a tonal and genuine "self," free to cross plateaus in the rhizomatic maneuvering and "becoming" (*TP* 162). *Anti-Oedipus* seeks a rhizomatic cultural production of "the self" (and its desires) in late-capitalist culture—allowing for a Nietzschean perspectival resistance to desire as a centralized social agency. The schiz, without ego, serves as a point of departure (*AO* xix). The schizophrenic subject embraces the erasure of the ego, the site of neurosis and the production of desire in late-capitalism. *Anti-Oedipus* seeks to discover deterritorialized flows of desire (those not mapped out by repression and neuroticized coding). The schizoid flows are forces that escape commercial coding, scramble ideological codes, and may lead to new social arrangements: nomads (no territories).

In "reading" any text, one real(izes) it to be an ideological product. One can never engage with the text as an individual—s/he always brings to it the signs, codes, and markers of the collective consciousness of our society, since we are all unable to escape the historical-cultural significance of the sign. What readers see through the "eyes" of William's text is the rupture of a reality in which no meaning exists outside the sociohistorical influence of the sign. The text purposefully works on the fringe of the ideological constructs of our sign system, often playing with the signs and symbols of this ideological system and disrupting our sociosemiotic placement of (our)selves within it. With its disregard for traditional literary conventions of plot fragmentation, paragraphing, syntax, and so forth, its superimposition of archaic symbols onto modern photography, and its presentation of bizarre settings juxtaposed with familiar images of the cross, the work plays at the cultural boundaries between center and margin, madness and reason, literature and nonliterature. Located in this unresolved area between boundaries, such schizoid discourse is, at once, both outside of the present sign system and within a "field" where meaning is being spontaneously created (Other). As conscious subjects (monitoring screens), readers are placed within this field and are constantly forced to reflect, accept, reject, and create as they go. Nomadic in nature, this frontier text deterritorializes the ideological and semiological placement of the subject and brings about new systems (plateaus) of existence and new ways for the subject to semantically locate it(s)elf in the world (i.e., "read").

Reading *A Pair of Eyes* continually repositions the subject (in process) throughout an ideological network of signification and implodes what is recognized as social reality, thereby offering the reader varying lines of flight into new social plateaus. The text offers a fictive corporeality that renders traditional identity and subjectivity unstable. It begins by turning the subject into a lexical identity, circulating it through the iconic markers of late-capitalist desires, and depicts the progression of the "subject" through historically overdetermined images of a cultural past. These images include our nation at war (World War II, Civil War, and news photos from Vietnam) technology and industry, Homer, the Declaration of Independence, Pac Man, and television. This experience ultimately leads to "hyperheteroglossia"—a bombardment of cross-s(t)imulation from messages of different sociohistorical positions and ideological discourses. As such, William's text transmogrifies the sign-system by "overcoding" ultimate levels of signification. In doing so, it dislocates the centers of ideological networks of power/signification and disrupts the ways in which ideological discourse(s) create our conscious reality.

A Pair of Eyes begins with a blank page and proceeds to create a consciousness for us. A quote from Lao Tzu appears before the body of the text: "Cut out doors and windows in order to make a room. Adapt the nothing therein to the purpose at hand, and you will have use of the room." This is an invitation for us to define our consciousness beginning from an unconscious. Beginning with unconsciousness is significant because according to Jacques Lacan, the unconscious is the only place where an authentic, or nonscripted "self" may exist. Authenticity is impossible to ascertain, however, since an entry into symbolic language is necessary before "the self" can ever realize its true unscriptedness. Consequently, the text proceeds to create a consciousness that is hypersignified as *subject to* culture, ultimately deconstructing the material/historical "self" through the text.

Throughout, waking and going from darkness into light is the dominant metaphor; pages begin by placing us in night and then bringing us into the light, as if bringing a consciousness to light for us. A consciousness is verbally created using ideological signifiers such as "war," "capitalism," "classes," "quarter pounders," "dollar signs," and "America." On page 0, the reader is asked to "be only a pair of eyes and to glance into a field of common memory." This glancing is into a collective reality—one always already present and defined through a complex network of social relations and discourses. Williams writes that "the *screen* will come, from her own tradition [italics mine]." It is a pluralistic tradition, comprised of the historical, literary, ideological, economic, and political images of our screenal culture: "The mind responds automatically, filling the moment with the beginning of an image" (1). The historical, material image supplied by culture manifests in some sign form (screen) via language. Readers are created as "selves" in the text, one word or image after another on the page: "I am one word after another on the page" (20), and later: "Take the images faster, let the word become a body" (27). At one point Williams asks: "Where are you between the images?" (19).

Today, the subject is constantly transformed into a "screen" coded with the cultural logic of the sign. Charles Levin states in "Carnal Knowledge of Aesthetic States":

> [A]s our rationalist and schizoid ego impulse would lead us to believe, and even to wish, then the temporalization of the sign, and consequent failure of the ideal, traps the meaning of being-alive-now in the scrutiny of the screen memory of the signifier.... The signifier, or screen memory, condenses an absence that compels us, and we are hypnotized by the prospect of a personal significance in the apparently random constellations of effects before us. (103)

In the telecommunicative ecstasy of proliferating cultural imagery, the simultaneously subject/object Man becomes "overcoded" (tattooed) and historically schizophrenic (Pfohl 71). As Baudrillard acknowledges: "The schizophrenic cannot produce the limits of his very being.... He becomes a pure screen" (*EC* 27).

On a most elementary level in the text, this dislocation of the postmodern (screenal) "self" takes place first in the form of primitive images and at the level of the sign. Many of the pages in the text contain photographs or prints overlaid with numerous archaic figures and iconographic images. Following page 3, is a silhouette of a human figure running through an abyss toward a primitive image (actually a reverse of a detail of a still from the Pudovkin film *Matka*). Later in the text, a detail of Ray Charles's face is juxtaposed with this image, screaming as though it(s)elf were becoming distorted in the Lacanian process of signification, through which the desiring-subject is simultaneously constituted and alienated by its entry into the symbolic. At another point in the text, Indian writing and a cross symbol appear beside the ancient Chinese symbol of the macrocosm, the Yin and Yang. Here, the text reaches outside of our culture's sign system and places a familiar image adjacent to unfamiliar ones, forcing the reader to fill the subsequent gaps. As subjectivity reaches a point of aesthetic excess, overcoded with hypersignified images, the individual enters into the aporias and sites of rupture in the text—that is, the aphanesthetic subject falls into the folds of simulacra.

Throughout, the text demystifies social rites, icons, and markers. Williams writes: "Today we are entering into the opening of an image, the whirling back in a counterclockwise motion into the symbol of the cross" (27). The inclusion of many "primal" images that preceded modern culturally inscribed ones serves to demake history, to descript culture, and to dematerialize the images that constitute subjectivity. Williams writes: "An image is turning over and over in my mind on its journey back into silence" (14). Intersecting with past familiar images are a number of contemporary ones: pictures of destroyed power lines, prisoners of war in bondage, and advertisements. By juxtaposing these modern images with archaic ones—placing them in new and ironic contexts—the text denaturalizes them all for us. We are dislocated amid these images and freed to progress as "reading" subjects through the text. Williams writes: "Images connect together in momentary resonances—opening from visible to invisible. . . .—*nothing matters and everything depends on this one moment*" (21). This is the moment of pure subjectivity, where, like for the schizophrenic, signifiers lose their signifieds and become literal images, representing nothing more than themselves (Jameson 120). According to Jameson, the "schizophrenic experience is an experience of isolated, disconnected, discontinuous material signifiers" (119). Through these experiences, consciousness regresses to undo social markers that have been inscribed on us, a process that enables us to enter an asymbolic space, that potential space of free subjectivity.

A Pair of Eyes succeeds in pushing the contemporary accumulation of signs to a point of excess—into hyperlogic—just as our entertainment culture today bombards us with signs from past and present mass media. Ultimately, this reiteration of images in the text disembodies the reader from the bondage of corporeal semiotics, leaving only the materiality of the sign to reflect itself. By alienating the sign readers are forced to take it "literally," as nothing more than a sign, driving the regime of the sign toward its own logical self-destruction (Harland 182). In the process, the material coding system of our culture is itself disembodied. In such a manner, the text deconstructs the ideological construction of the subject-self in terms of our culture, opening up rhizomatic lines of flight that resist culturally coded "desires" and capitalist inscriptions (consumption as sign, identity, body, etc.). Williams writes: "I de-make this book, and, in the motion of return, the ending becomes a beginning branching into the unseen" (28) Such a "schizoid" ethics is a post-modern pragmatics of survival, a "drift" beyond the palimpsest of (his)torical simulacra to an ahistorical continuum of subjectivity.

Chapter Six

Desire, Seduction, and Subjectivity in Kathy Acker's Novels: *Blood and Guts in High School* and *Don Quixote*

> Seducing for a woman consists in sliding into an empty place, where her ideal form is already traced out by all those of her sex who have preceded her.
>
> —Jean Baudrillard, *Cool Memories*

> The entire contemporary history of the body is the history of its demarcation, the network of marks and signs that have since covered it, divided it, and annihilated its difference and its radical ambivalence in order to organize it into a structural material for sign-exchange, equal to the sphere of objects....
>
> —Jean Baudrillard, *Symbolic Exchange and Death*

Kathy Acker's work, like that of the other writers explored here, reappropriates those textual sights overcoded by (His)tory. The occurrence of (His)tory as a simulacrum might better be seen as the male-coded text of gender identities and bodies fatally (always already) inscribed for their subjects by the complex network of socializing and commercializing forces, also called "phallogocentrism." In rewriting the phallogocentric text, her work (most especially *Don*

Quixote) is similar in manner to the multimedia work done by Critical Art Ensemble (CAE) that appropriates technology and reinscribes it into the body (through the overlaying of images and signs, or other forms of telecritical performance) to disrupt the cultural coding of the body-text through the same medium (digital technologies, media, and cinema) by which it is ritually doubled. Anti-institutional in nature, these works deterritorialize desire, identity, and the body by reappropriating and resigning them (Smith 69). Whereas Critical Art Ensemble reinscribes technology into the body in performances such as "BwO (body without organs) Now," Acker, through a headlong flight into (and out of) phallocracy, seeks out points of rupture of "desire" in any phallogocentric text, making possible a radical break between regimes of signs and their objects and evoking a vision of female subjectivity in a nomadic mode. As Brian Massumi posits: "bodies in flight do not leave the world behind . . . they take the world with them into the future" (105).

This chapter on Acker reinterprets the fatal motions of postmodernity in which "humanity" and "sexuality" are possessed and tattooed with patriarchal images of a technological simulacrum wherein a violent doubling (coding) is done to the body-made-text, identity-made-commodity, and "code-made-flesh" (*PI* 64). Women are aesthetically raped every day on prime-time TV in jeans ads and beer commercials that return to be reified in the behavior patterns of men at the bar or fraternity house that evening. Hence, hyperaesthetics as the production of images and consumption of signs, no more evident than the glamour, advertising, and media industries that "inscribe the surface of the body, its *tattoo*, as a text for the playing out of the commodity form as power" (Kroker *PI* 17).

Body Invaders, edited by Arthur Kroker, is a collection of essays that analyze the laceration of the body by the political economy of signs—fashion, TV, or the modern BwO (electronic dispersion of the body across the mediascape). Jean Baudrillard says that under these (His)torical conditions: "the body has been reduced to a division of surfaces, a proliferation of multiple objects . . . a fractal body which can no longer hope for resurrection" (*EC* 44). Not only is there the social overcoding of the subject, but the "virtual body" as well becomes a site of subjugated knowledge: "the vision of power as a body invader inscribing itself on the text of the flesh; and theorizing the possibility of a margin of difference which would transgress the grisly play of power which is always only topical and relational" (*PS* 25). In this hyperreal equation, patriarchal power is always put into play as code, "through a relentless exteriorization of the faculties of the body, and through a surrealistic resymbolization of the text of lived experience" (*PS* 75). The phallic code (in late-capitalist consumer culture) is fortified as the body doubles into signs (*SE&D* 106). At this technological site—technology as an instrument of social exploitation and physical domination—one finds both the telemetried body and the ideologically interpolated subject positioned somewhere on the postmodern grid of power/seduction, within the circulated images and signs of desire (*PS* 26).

Acker's writing presents a three-way intersection between power/seduction/desire, where Baudrillard again meets Giles Deleuze and Felix Guattari. A Deleuzian strategy for reading her works offers a schizophrenic line of flight through desire and language to escape the coding of our *molar selves* in contemporary culture. This motion brings with it friction to that societal body of representations. The Deleuzian critic Brian Massumi asserts that molar men, or the man-form that dominates our culture (patriarchy, or the ideal of reason), must "[d]e-form themselves. Dissociate their bodies and desires from the apparatus of overcoding that has up to now defined them, and forced complementary definitions on other in their name" (89). In *Don Quixote*, Acker writes: "this exploitation or reduction of reality to self-preservation and the manipulable other has become the universal principle of a society which seeks to reduce all phenomena to this enlightenment, ideal of rationalism, or subjugation of other" (72). Because it is unlikely that the "masculine" will easily surrender its privileged position "their suicide may have to be assisted" (Massumi 89). Following this Deleuzian lead, critics such as Douglas Dix call Acker's disjunctive and dramatic prose technique a drastic revolutionary method for transforming society (opening thought to new plateaus), one that takes a "nomadic" shape in works such as *Don Quixote*. As Massumi puts it: "'Nomad thought' does not lodge itself in the edifice of an ordered interiority; it moves freely in an element of exteriority"(5). Rosi Braidotti praises Acker's "visceral passion for nomadic transformations and her Deluzian flair for the reversibility of situations and people—her borderline capacity to impersonate, mimic, and cut across an infinity of 'others'" (28). Woman, as universal subject of *becoming*, might be revolutionary if in the process it were possible to create a non-Oedipal woman (*desire* as affirmative) and "to the extent that they develop a consciousness that is not specifically feminine, dissolving 'woman' into the forces [symbolic, sociological, and physical] that structure her. The ultimate aim is to achieve not a sex-specific identity but rather the dissolution of identity into an impersonal, multiple, machinelike subject" (116). Acker's works often present this very sort of subjectivity and speak to its sociosymbolic trappings.

In contrast, according to Baudrillard, seduction offers resistance, a "disguise for survival," against the edifying late-capitalist economies of desire, where signs of love, sexuality, and the body have all entered the sphere of hyperexchange value (*BL* 47-48). In a "world of appearances (*DQ* 130), the feminine capacity to challenge masculine representation lies with seduction, which has the power within a universe of symbolic exchange values, where "all qualities have been and are reduced to quantitative equivalences" (*DQ* 72), and according to which sexuality, power, and the body are all produced as simulated desires. In this economy, sex becomes the actualization of desire in pleasure (not love); you have a body, and a sexual drive, and you must expend it (*SED* 38). For Baudrillard, sexuality, the body, desire, and love all appear in Western culture as capital relations:

This pressure towards liquidity, flux and the accelerated articulation of the sexual, psychic and physical body is an exact replica of that which regulates exchange value: capital must circulate, there must no longer be any fixed point, investments must be ceaselessly renewed, value must radiate without respite—this is the form of value's present realization, and sexuality, the sexual *model*, is simply its mode of appearance at the level of the body. (*SED* 38)

There is a productive form of the economy of sex and the body that invades and inscribes every facet of desire as a simulacrum of late-capitalism. Sex, today, occurs not only within the institutions of psychoanalysis and biomedicine that map every possible terrain of corporeal, conscious, and unconscious desire ("self"), but also at the hands of the cosmetic and fashion industries and the media that corroborate and validate the process of simulation. Feminine desire is simulation: "Femininity manifests itself as an abstract totality, devoid of any reality it can call its own, a product of the discourse and rhetoric of advertising" (*SED* 92). That is, in the ideology of a consumer-culture materialism, the female is alienated by a "femininity" that is parasitical to the simulational beauty and fashion industries, "subjecting her body to the reproduction of capital" (*SED* 92). Moreover, at this interface between sexuality and power where woman finds her(self) transformed into image by the gaze, she simultaneously reinforces the representational industry's coding system while being excluded from the masculine production of signs.

Consider the selling of Lulu by Shigold, the white slave trader who claims to be her father in *Don Quixote*. The governor, who buys/marries her, and becomes her daddy remarks: "you see: you're a whore. You're a toilet men use, an empty hallway any men wander in and out of. You are nothing" (*DQ* 88). Consumer society, writes Mike Gane: "confers on the object [an] imaginary quality of the feminine, to be 'available at will'" (152), where the masculine role is to produce, to fill (with representations), to mark, and to possess or control. This is the pornographic quality of the object: to be totally present, totally accessible to the patriarchal gaze: "Pornography's 'oeuvre' is a surplus of phallic investment on the body; a textual disinvestment of the body's essential power and the management of sexual difference; ultimately, a pathetic exposure of the representational nature of desire" (Kaite 165). The revenge of the feminine, then, is to enter the hyperreal dimension of pornographic fascination (to transform themselves into the pure object) that always requires "proof of capacity" and renders masculine desire vulnerable (Gane 151). Here, Baudrillard suggests the power of seduction: "By applying their makeup, they make themselves into a pure appearance, denuded of meaning. . . . The seduction, fascination and 'aesthetic' attraction of all the great imaginary processes lies here: in the effacing of every instance, be it the face and every substance, be it desire—in the artificial perfection of the sign" (*SED* 94). The feminine capacity for deception (and power) lies in the seduction and learning how to manipulate the (symbolic) world of appearances. By transforming herself into pure play of marks and signs (of desire) on the surface, the feminine may procure a pure line of flight into the BwO (free of "lips," "tits," and "cunts" [Acker]) and expropriate masculine authority or phallic investment of the body. According to Baudrillard, to seduce masculine desire, we must seize the "strategy of appearances," which women alone hold (*SED* 8): "women have been dispossessed [given over to the code] of their bodies, their desires, happiness, and rights. But they have always remained mistresses of . . . seductive disappearance and translucence, and so have always been capable of eclipsing the power of their masters" (*SED* 88). To sacrifice the body to pure appearance (hypersexual pornography in Acker's works) serves to challenge the semiurgical colonization of the topos of the body by participating in its object: "seduction can today reinvent these forces, and raise them against the terrorist seizing of truth and verification, of identification and programming which engulf us" (*EC* 75). This challenge to the dominant order of the gaze is the power immanent to seduction—to side with the object (always already the feminine order), because "fatal strategies can only be launched from the side of the object" (Gane 66).

In *The Ecstasy of Communication*, Baudrillard declares: "Seduction is an invention of stratagems, of the body, as a disguise for survival, as an infinite dispersion of lures, as an art of disappearance and absence, as a dissuasion which is stronger yet than that of the system" (75). Fashion, which, today, must signify the body (as the play of signs on its surface) can serve as a neutralizer of sexuality and, therefore, precipitate the body-as-object's disappearance (*SE&D* 96). As Baudrillard points out: "What is inescapable is not desire, but the ironic presence of the object, its indifference and indifferent connections, its challenge, its seduction, and its disobedience to the symbolic order" (*FS* 182). To oppose the phallocentric structure, the women's movement has erred by stressing "difference, a specificity of desire and pleasure, a different relation to the female body, speech, and writing but *never seduction*" (*SED* 8). According to Baudrillard: "[feminists] do not understand *that seduction represents mastery over the symbolic universe, while power represents only mastery of the real universe*"(*SED* 8). The (now) secondary order of the real has long been transformed into the order of simulation—everything is made to appear real (Coke, veneer coffee tables, TV shows—i.e., *The Real World*. The feminine trait of seduction has the capacity to control the symbolic (primary) order of exchange at the level of appearances and antagonize the (illusory) masculine principles of the real, authenticity, and depth (Gane 145). An appropriation of desire by the object, "launched from the side of the object," via seductive complicity subsumes the symbolic order in which these repressive and institutionalizing categories of masculine "truth" are produced. Seduction is always and in every sense opposed to production (which is the order of desire) (*SED* 34). It effaces and absorbs symbolic power: "Seduction removes something from the order of the visible, while production constructs everything in full view" (*SED* 34). Production is the order of masculine desire—of objects, of bodies, of truth, knowledge, and discourse, all forms of real(ity). The discourse of sexual desire (as labor, truth, and the real) is produced by the dominant (simulation) order and circulated. By parading these apparent "truths," through her brutally obscene descriptions of sexual acts and pornographic (immediate, total, and transparent) depictions of women's bodies on sexual display, Acker subverts the masculine order of production.

Our hyperreal fascination with the pornographic (wars so close we can watch them from our living rooms, death so close there are movies compiled from home videos: *Faces of Death I, II, and III*), ushers in a new state of obscenity for America. In pornography, one encounters the more true than true, the more real than real, the more sexual than sexual (*SED* 78). Here:

> Everything is to become real, visible, accountable; everything is to be transcribed in relations of force, systems of concepts or measurable energy; everything is to be said, accumulated, indexed and recorded. This is sex as it exists in pornography, but more generally, this is the enterprise of our entire culture, whose natural condition is obscene: a culture of monstration, of demonstration, of productive monstrosity. (*SED* 35)

What is pornographic is not only bodies involved in copulation, but the redundancy of sex to the "nth" power. In pornography, the image is seen for what it is: "the product of a generic set of representational codes and images" (224). It may be that the *obscene* nature of Acker's works neutralizes masculine representations of desire (sex and death), which is the power of seduction.

So, against the late forms of representational desire (masculine models of sign production) which have developed through the commercialization and exploitation of women's bodies (especially apparent in the advertising industry since the 1950s), Baudrillard poses obscenity: "obscenity as an enticement, and thus as an 'indefinable' allusion to desire. An obscenity too brutal to be true, and too impolite to be dishonest—obscenity as a challenge, and therefore, again, as seduction" (*SED* 43). It is the only strategy left for participation in a society without depth. As Gane puts it: "What was dominant here was not the principle of love and happiness, but that of the (deadly) game of seduction and counter-seduction, at the level of pure appearance" (58). Certainly, Acker's novels depict this sort of generalized pornographic culture, where (hyperreal) love and happiness exist (if anywhere) on TV sets in coffee ads and soap operas, and sex is accessed through telephone lines from television and magazine ads. Acker's world is the apogee of obscenity and pornography: there is no room for illusion; everything is transparently real; and everything becomes political, cultural, and given over to meaning (the body, identity, and sexuality)—the absolute proximity of sex and death. Hers is a world exhausted of meaning—a disenchanted world of indifferent ecstasy, panic sex without desire, the body stripped of its appearances (beyond the signifying sphere of fashion). A perfectly ecstatic and obscene universe of pure objects is offered to a masculine ocular penetration, and in total irony.

Seduction is rejected by many gyno-feminists, who want to locate the truth of woman in her body and her desires, but in fact that "truth" is always already in the realm of the object, foremost processed through a masculine (pornographic) will. Women's bodies, identity, gender, value are inescapably phallocentric products processed through (object to) the male text of "desire" (as simulacrum). Examine the word, "S/he," always already embedded in male textuality, or "Wo/man" as a receptacle of the masculine "will" (scripted). The pornographic, or disenchanted, form of the body (without seduction) is a product of the phallic order: the "written" body is always the object that the masculine text imposes its "will" or desires upon (inscribes). The (dis)simulation of woman/object/truth occurs because everything is imbued with interpretation (redoubles); it is always already derived from the order of masculine desire. The seduction of the object is that it knows it is always already simulated (as apparent truth), which it always conceals (like woman). Desire may be only a masculine myth—a will to power that seduction, in "forming a web of appearances," can exorcise (*SED* 87). When seducing, the woman realizes her body and desires are not her own, and so plays with them (*SED* 86). Because she does not own her body: "she turns herself into a pure appearance, an artificial construct with which to trap the desires of others. Seduction consists in letting the other believe himself to be the subject of his desire, without oneself being caught in this trap" (*SED* 86). To desire is actually to become the destiny of the other, turning the subject into the object (*FS* 114). Acker's works seize on this irony and turn "desire" in on itself, reversing the enslaving signs of phallogocentrism through seduction: "Seduction alone breaks the distinctive sexualization of bodies and the inevitable phallic economy that results . . . it is there all at once, in the reversal of all the alleged depth of the real, of all psychology, anatomy, truth, or power. It knows (and this is its secret) that *there is no anatomy*, nor psychology, that all signs are reversible. Nothing belongs to it, except appearances" (*SED* 10).

According to Baudrillard, woman has always defined this space of artifice, of simulation, of authentic inauthenticity, of appearances (Gane 148). And this is the secret of her seductive strength—not to embed desire, but to allow an obese proliferation of pornographic and prostituted signs of desire "appearing" everywhere to thwart the masculine depth. This is

> [t]he capacity immanent to seduction to deny things their truth and turn it into a game, the pure play of appearances, and thereby foil all systems of power and meaning with a mere turn of the hand. The ability to turn appearances in on themselves, to play on the body's appearances, rather than with the depths of desire. Now all appearances are reversible . . . only at the level of appearances are systems fragile and vulnerable . . . meaning is vulnerable only to enchantment. (*SED* 8)

To seduce is to invert reality, to become deception, an illusory image in which others will be caught; it has the ability to confuse itself with the production of reality and desire, which operates under the fundamental illusion of the sign (*SED* 69). Seduction occurs in the absorption of empty, senseless signs. It is at a point of saturation, transparency, and fascination that seduction can escape a signified (masculine) desire. It is precisely this obsessive and traumatic site in Acker's works—where disjunctive signs, images, and dreams interplay in a continuous sense of irony—that the (pornographic) signs of male-produced desire (phallocracy) appearing everywhere break from their referents, and "desire's" absence (appearing only in simulation) is most surely felt.

In nothing less than a true "empire of the senseless," [1] in the ceaseless demonstration, simulation, and pornography of our culture (sex sells everything from automobiles to Hooters chicken wings), one experiences an exhaustion that diffuses and neutralizes sexuality. In Acker's works depicting overproduced, hypersignified, and prostituted sexuality, masculinity loses out and confronts impotence. The obscene and direct sexual invitation, "fuck me," serves as a challenge to masculine desire and gender and, therefore, as a seduction. Baudrillard contends that "[t]he feminine is not just seduction; it also suggests a challenge to the male to be the sex, to monopolize the sex and sexual pleasure, a challenge to go to the limits of its hegemony and exercise it unto death. Today, phallocracy is collapsing under the pressure of this challenge. . . . Our entire conception of sexuality may be collapsing because constructed around the phallic function" (*SED* 21). Feminine seduction poses a challenge that can reverse the masculine order of the sign and provide a space free of referentiality to desire—a space of violent play and militant defiance to invert male sexual force (*SED* 21). At this point, the masculine is mastered by its own pornographic image. Baudrillard holds that

> today, behind the mechanical objectification of the signs of sex, it is the masculine as fragile, and the feminine as degree zero which have the upper hand . . . [a] violence done the "subsuicidal" male by unbridled female sensualism . . . and the collapse of the marked term by the irruption of the unmarked term. It is not real, generic violence, but the violence of dissuasion, the *violence of the neuter*, the violence of degree zero. (*SED* 27)

In its ironic from, seduction breaks the reference to sex and desire and moves to ludicy, hence challenge. Nowhere is the seductive strategy of (dis)simulation more explosive and striking than in the works of Acker, wherein the signs of obscenity and pornography are doubled against the capitalist phallocratic order of simulation that produces them.

Acker's *Blood and Guts in High School* depicts the contemporary experiences of women that are seldom heard by articulating the violence upon the female subject/object (a distinction that is ambiguous to the heroine Janey, who inherently knows that even as subject, she is always already the pornographic object of male voyeurism). Acker accomplishes this effect by processing her characters (fragmented, manipulated, and exploited) through the masculine discourses of desire in late-capitalist culture. In the novel, Janey is enslaved by her emotional and physical need for love and sex with her boyfriend-Father, and by a language imbued with patriarchal definitions that equate love and sex, as "fuck love." She exists within a system of interpersonal relations by which her identity as a woman is kept in bondage, and by which she is made to desire that bondage. Under a drawing of a woman's torso, legs spread exposing her vagina, Acker writes: "Girls will do anything for love" (*B&GHS* 62). (On a lesser scale, consider the number of women who annually put their health at risk by receiving breast implants or by wearing high-heeled shoes, for that matter.) Janey's desperation to attain love overrides all other desires "cause she wanted to fuck love more than she felt pain" (*B&GHS* 21). Acker brutally tells us that love and sexuality in America is capitalistic S&M, the "glorification" of "slavery and prison." Besides reality, love, sex, and fucking, have all been made into instruments of exploitation and domination in a mechanical sign-slide by our materialistic society that does away with feelings for a value of exchange (*B&GHS* 99). Commenting on the late-capitalist commodification of all spheres, Baudrillard writes: "Under the sign of the commodity, love becomes prostitution" (*SE&D* 108). Near the end of the novel, Acker expresses this entrapment: "Being in prison is being in a cunt. Having any sex in the world is having to have sex with capitalism" (*B&GHS* 135).

Imprisoned by the Arab white-slave traders, Janey learns of the economy of her body (inscribed "whore")—the exchange value of her "cunt" for male desire (*B&GHS* 65). She *literally* discovers her value "phallogocentrically" in the Persian language she acquires in the closet. Janey's body is made a prison to men's wills: "My cunt used to be a men's toilet," she says (*B&GHS* 36). Through the reappropriation of the metaphor "cunt" as the "repulsive hole," "red, ugly, ugh" (*B&GHS* 19), Acker hypersignifies and, in the process, dislocates the violence of male desire and its ownership of the female subject as exploited sexual object in the cultural text. What one witness in Acker's novels is a sacrificial culture that will create thousands of anorexic women a year in America for the sake of selling their double: the cosmetic industry fuels the fashion industry, which fuels the diet pill industry, which fuels the feminine hygiene market. There is little difference between the white-slave traders' language and the semiology of the male-dominated fashion, beauty, and hygiene industries that sell images of women every day on television.

As much as they deal with masculine desire, Acker's texts also concern the political and religious restraints of female desire. Throughout her writing, female desire explodes as an anarchic response to the dominant ideology (although it's *fatal*), because she realizes, as Deleuze and Guattari note, that "If desire is repressed, it is because every position of desire, no matter how small, is capable of calling into question the established order of a society" (*AO* xxiii). In this light, one might term her "rhizomatic" work as a *feminist* one that remaps the culturally, politically, and religiously determined (owned) lines of the feminine body. In this vein, Kroker asks:

> For what has feminist theory always been about if not a refusal of the grand metaphysics of Being, of the unitary of the male subject, of the phallocentric order of the Subject, Species, Membership; in favor of "multiplicities," of a dancing materiality of lines of flight and departure; of a world re-enchanted by the language of desire? Not the old boring world of phallocentric oppositions, but liquid doublings where the body finally speaks ... [w]here, that is, a new language is articulated which is capable of addressing both the disappearance of women under the sign of despotic power: the material language of markings, of deterritorialization and dematerialization, of gestural signatures; and of inscribing a new feminist possibility.... The feminist subject, then, as an event-scene, living at the edge of the material body and virtual reality. Neither really pure corporeal denotation or perfect virtuality or desire; but both simultaneously. A "virtual feminism" which is a matter of decodings (the "multiplicities" in the relational world of the virtual self) and resignifications (the re-enchantment of bodily desire). (*PI* 119)

In the novel, Janey's dependency on sadomasochistic sex/love both defines her(self) as subject and as object (her body is an inscribed surface of events in a relational field of power). This dependency parodies, and hence retraces in language, the locus of the dissociated (virtual) female "self" that everywhere today adopts the illusion of unity provided by the image-producing industries (advertising, fashion, cinema, etc.). In this way, Acker's character rebels against the ideologically and commercially coded restraints that operate on women at all levels of social, political, and personal interaction.

As a kind of rhizomatic maneuvering, Acker forges obscenity and pornography into a radical narrative form to upset the language structure, because these discourses are outside society's accepted handling of sexuality. On the other hand, pornography can be reappropriated as the language of women because they have always been objectified as sexual commodities. In Acker's novels, women's longing to be desiring subjects only leads to death (i.e., to desire love is to desire to become the sexual object of men's desire). Women are denied a subject position in language. Addressing "Dog," Medusa remarks: "I'm your desire's object, dog. Because I can't be the subject. Because I can't be the subject: What you name 'love,' I name 'nothingness' ... Why? Objects can't love back" (*DQ* 28). So Acker's characters become what they must, pure (pornographic) objects. As Baudrillard puts it: "Exhibition is the perfect form of obscenity. That is what gives it its power" (*BL* 47). The sexual exploitation of women has taught them to feel like prisoners of their bodies and to use their bodies for economy in patriarchal culture (*DQ* 167). Janey cries: "I've been so repressed in this crummy room like a prison every day doing less and less and thinking more and more until something's going to break, probably my body" (*B&GHS* 59). Women have been made slaves of their bodies and emotions as they have been defined by pain and economy in our society. And they have been made to feel that their only value is sexual. Acker writes: "Body Slavery:

I have to eat and get shelter so need money. Also, my body likes sex and also rich food and I'll do anything for those" (*B&GHS* 111).

In our culture, women have been forced into a sadomasochistic economy of value. Acker's formal use of pornography illustrates the sexual violence that women have come to appreciate as their value: Janey says: "I told him to get a belt. I think I shocked him. He took a heavy leather belt and whipped me across the back as he fucked me in the ass. It hurt almost too much and I liked it" (*B&GHS* 59). The pain and indignation in Acker's work forces us to recognize the suppression of women's identity and voice as (His)torically and psychologically related directly to male violence (social, political, sexual, and textual). Janey can never decide whether or not she is "a self" or an object, since "selves" are supposed to love, which for her is the experience of being objectified, abused, hurt, and denied—a receptacle of capitalist mapping and victimizing. She wishes there was a "reason to believe" the letter "I" (*B&GHS* 108). Ultimately, Janey learns that "Women aren't just slaves. They are whatever their men want them to be. They are made, created by men. They are nothing without men" (*B&GHS* 130). Since women have no language, psychology, or bodies of their own, since they have no reality or identity apart from men, they are like dogs. ("Dogs" speak metaphorically for the dehumanizing of women throughout the novel, *Don Quixote*.) Since women can't love, they can't exist (*DQ* 161). For a woman to free herself from her culturally "marked" body would be to lose all definition (mother, whore, bitch, cunt, model, and prostitute), to become nothing (*DQ* 153). In essence, without the (mis)representations of women that language holds, women would be nothing in the phallogocentric order.

At a stylistic level, Acker's works serve to disrupt and deface the entire patriarchal tradition, especially the formal elements of conventional literary centers in narrative fiction. Richard Walsh calls her writing "tableaux"; she uses a "spatial model of the novel" to establish coherent positions and "signif icant thematic relationships between disparate textual fragments" (151). Her narratives are made of nonlinear, discontinuous, and cyclic plots that often progress to points of disarticulation: genders reverse, fathers become boyfriends, and objects become subjects. Commenting on her style in *Don Quixote*, Walsh writes: "Acker's use of this reiterative, episodic narrative model allows her to introduce multiple subnarratives: the continuity of the text is a function of thematic characteristics and the quest framework she takes from Cervantes: its substance has the freedom of extreme discontinuity [that] creates a plurality of textual articulations and subverts any monolithic narratorial identity" (163). On another level, her writing confounds both high and low elements of the dominant culture. She borrows from and incorporates all sorts of cultural texts into her writing: diagrams, scrawlings and "obscene" drawings, fragments of dreams and poetry, Shakespeare, political commentary, popmusic (the artist formerly known as Prince), and pornography. In this sense,

Acker's plagiarized version of writing serves to challenge all authoritative versions of the social texts as being themselves nothing more than powerful fictive representations. Moreover, she reverses the phallocentric penetration of a masculine cultural voice into the female by hypersignifying that text, and in the process, denigrates the violent disruption of the phallus into the vagina. This occurs, literally, as her writing offensively smacks us in the face with these images (father fucking Janey, slave trader raping Janey, Dog being beaten) as well as metaphorically, such as when Janey and Don Quixote enter into "maddened" searches for "love" in a world of indenturing representations.

Don Quixote (its plagiarized title bearing a postmodern belief in the nihilistic argument that there is nothing new) subverts the simulacra of masculine desire in traditional male discourse. By incorporating the narrative structure of Miguel de Cervantes's *Don Quixote* into her novel, Acker avoids the postmodern propensity to aimlessness and counters the apparent nihilism of her project. Whereas Cervantes's borrowings sought to parody the chivalric romance, Acker's plagiarism of the plot structure of Cervantes's novel undermines not only the entire foundation of the canonical masculine romance-quest but indicts along with it a culture that operates from the vantage point of male desire. The goal for Acker's hero-knight (who is female as opposed to male) is to acquire sexual desire in heterosexual love for women (i.e., reverse the masculine order of signs). Acker subverts the masculine notion of love (as conquest) and desire (as possession) by illustrating that to be "loved," for a woman, is to be put through, or "suffer," the male text (simulations) of desire, of sexual exchange, torture, abuse, and death—making explicit the "victimizing" force of female desire in a masculine culture. Ours is a culture in which women strive to manifest in themselves the perfection "defined" in pictures of Revlon supermodels ("Cover Girl: Redefining Beauty") simply to attain male attention and gratify a longing for companionship, a desire that results in nothing less than a loss of individuality as one's identity is feigned from the masculine constructs of the fashion and cosmetic industries and represented through TV images. (Barbie dolls are still leading sellers on the Home Shopping Network, as successful as their spectral look-alike actresses on sitcoms, soap operas, and at the movies.) Fittingly, the heroine (k)night of the novel can only aspire to be victimized and to sacrifice her feminine identity in the quest for "real" love as the male defines it. Men own, rule, and determine everything in our society (including language). Ultimately, in a white-male-capitalist culture of double standards in morality, greed, and materialism as an ideology, and unequal power relations or "the subjugation of Other "(*DQ* 72), Don Quixote discovers that it is impossible for a woman to "love."

The entire novel reveals Don Quixote's aborted attempts to love, and her experience of becoming a knight who attempts to save the "man-made," or male-produced, world from its "real" love. "Real love" for Don Quixote is analogous to the sacrificial pain of abortions brought on by the impossible situations faced by women who desire love—pain caused by men, sex, and cultural representations of desire and love. On the examiner's table, Don Quixote remarks: "Hasn't loving a man brought me to this abortion or state of death?" (*DQ* 10). Abortions, writes Acker in *Blood and Guts in High School*, "are the symbol, the outer image, of sexual relations in this world. Describing my abortions is the only way I can tell you about pain and fear . . . my unstoppable drive for sexual love made me know" (*B&GHS* 34). Having the abortion puts Don Quixote in rebellion against the social values of her culture. The flow of blood from the abortion represents the woman's free-flowing sexuality and her rejection of social and religious (Catholic) authorities. Don Quixote must have the abortion that is representative of a pass beyond normalcy ("capitulation to social control"(*DQ* 18) to attain her (k)nighthood and search for love. By having the abortion, she reclaims her body and sexuality from the religious and political institutions and gains an identity. That is, she becomes a *desiring subject* who is able to search for love. Similarly, she must "abort" her femininity by entering into the masculine text to search for love (i.e., she must become the knight, a "normally" masculine identity, which is the *only* identity allowed to locate a subject position in our culture and search for love).

To escape cultural norms Don Quixote dreams of becoming a knight, so as to love and save the world—"which is the most insane idea any woman can think of" (*DQ* 10). The (k)night's visionary quest for an ideal and equitable form of love is an insane effort by society's standards, directed from the cultural margins at seeing through the "enchantment" of unequal power relations that the patriarchal tradition has forced us to accept as normal. Enchantment, Don Quixote says is to "have no choice and you must choose" (*DQ* 187). Don Quixote's only choices are to accept the male dominated culture (including its definitions of love) and be normalized into it, or stay outside of the culture and be considered insane. The language of the novel exudes this sense of despondency. Ironically, in reality, for women to love is an insane venture (*DQ* 9), one of masculine objectification, since heterosexual love often objectifies women. (Women are the object of domination and sexual acquisition.) Ultimately, the (k)night's quest is deemed insane because the entire male tradition would have to be turned topsy-turvy to allow women to love—that is, to become more than objects of male desire and to locate a subject position themselves from which to desire: "As long as you cling to a dualistic reality which is a reality molded by power, women will not exist with you" (*DQ* 28). Women would actually be transformed from dehumanized "dogs" into people for a different kind of love to evolve—one that is not centered on power but on equality. A double standard exists in love now: while men can simply desire women (which teaches women that their only value is sexual), females must desire to become the object of male desire and to enter into the order of sexual exchange value in a world of late-capitalist commodification. How can love be possible under capitalism in which there is always one party dominating another, requiring an exchange based on power that is always unequal? Acker writes: "You don't know how hellish capitalism really is. Daddy . . . I sucked cocks while their owners held guns to my head. . . . Love was rape and rejection. If I wasn't loved, I couldn't fit into this marketplace or world of total devaluation" (*DQ* 115). Women are taught that love is possession by men: "Because I love you I've destroyed myself . . . [Love] reverses subject and object" (*DQ* 51). By "loving" others Don Quixote neglects (her)self, and hence, negates her(self). Women can't love as a result of their constant battle between "self-appreciation" on one hand and socially taught sexual and moral ideals and gender-depiction constructs (Mrs. Cleaver or the Virgin Mary) on the other. These "ideals" (or "false consciousnesses") place women in the impossible position of being unable to fulfill them and, therefore, to suffer social castigation. In the novel, Catholic priests are called "thieves" and "evil enchanters" who create a contradictory and unattainable image for women (virgin-mother).

Women can't love because they cannot desire (or they are labeled "whores" by the male enchanters); they can only deny (men, their own sexual desires, their own identities, etc.). Don Quixote says of female identity that "[w]omen are bitches, dog. They're the cause of troubles between men and women. Why? because they don't give anything, they deny" (*DQ* 27). Denial is the only socially acceptable sexual role for women. Acker writes that a space should be opened for women as equals in our culture, to reappropriate the feminine subject and its desires from the bondage of male (His)tory and domination. When Don Quixote is being taught to appreciate her own bodily desires she remarks: "I'm forced to find a self when I've been trained to be nothing" (*DQ* 171). Yet, the novel is dystopic, because it appears to depict a failed quest from the onset, a ("mad") quest destined to end in death in the simulacra of male desire and definitions of love as "pain," "fucking," and "rage" in a brutally patriarchal ("real") culture: "All reality and madness are trying to destroy each other. Bam! Bam! Wop! Swop! Madness, because it's at thin old debilitated aborted night, is too weak. It had no chance of doing anything. . . . As it falls to the ground the invincible reality of malehood puts his sword to its pulsating heart" (*DQ* 33). Unable to find the ideal love of her visions in the male-enchanted world of "real" love that destroys women's identities, the (k)night is forced either to be "normalized" into a masculine order of love and desire (hence, allow her "visions" to die), or to "die" as a social individual (remain apart from the male world in her "madness"). Therefore, she confronts the following dilemma: "If a woman insists she can and does love and her living isn't loveless or dead, she dies. So either a woman is dead or she dies. . . . Can Don Quixote figure out how to love and live?' (*DQ* 33). Being female in a male world where women cannot love, Don Quixote is already dead; she is dead without language or sexuality, and, therefore, without a sense of self. Hence, the disruptive and disturbing text of *Don Quixote* itself depicts the fragmentary woman (observe the photo of Acker on its cover [2]) as a product of aborted efforts at love in that dominant culture. Somewhere between religious white men's prescriptions for sexuality, on one hand, and the advertising industry's representations of love, desire, and the body on the other, the female "self" as object is always already inscribed, or colonized, with the images and language of the dominant ideology.

At a semantic level, the novel appears as a graphic site of both personal and political violence against the female subject, making "love" into "fucking," "woman" into "cunt," and "me" into "body." Men have tried to change women "by simply lying, by saying that women live only for men's love. An alteration of language, rather than of material, usually changes material conditions" (*DQ* 27). The texts of both novels I've discussed respond to this violation with the use of disjunctive syntax and abrupt shifts in plot and points of view to indicate a violent reaction to the phallocentric logic, so as to, in a nomadic line of flight, reappropriate the linguistic space by which one might construct "identity," "self," "desire," or "love." Don Quixote speaks: "I wanted to find a meaning or myth or language that was mine, rather than those which try to control me; but language is communal and here is no community" (*DQ* 194). Without language one cannot exist. Don Quixote remarks: "I won't not be: I'll perceive and I'll speak" (*DQ* 28). Through its own molecular *becomings*, Acker's sentence structure fragments and decenters the textual subject and obliterates the semiotic social "authority" of the language that "marks" and binds the female. As Douglas Dix has experienced it: "The intense subjectivity of Acker's prose is itself a weapon of becoming" (57).

Ultimately, Acker's work makes epidemic the relation between "self," (His)tory, and culture. It portrays how the phallocentric text always serves to fragment and destroy female identity as it is processed through its definitions of reason, desire, power, and pleasure. As the dogs of the world (in this case women) and Don Quixote part at the conclusion of the novel, they sing a song to the (k)night that says: "because your human history which is the history of slavery is not our history, because your culture is slavery" (*DQ* 198) it must be rebelled against. (His)tory enslaves women within the simulacra it offers up for identity. Nevertheless, "(His)tory" means exactly what it implies, a fiction created by men that maintains their privilege position of tellers, as controllers of language ("landlords" who rule the world [*DQ* 199]). Language is a commodity, as is literature, and Acker's works are imbued with a sensibility that reappropriates language and literature by rewriting the *Don Quixote* myth, by rethinking love, and by repossessing the pornographic language that subjugates women to its possession. Acker realizes that the norms and laws of our culture that control love, desire, and sexuality are formed in a male language by the religious image makers and by the political myth makers who set the limits for female identity. She states: "What is the myth of America, for economic and political war or control now is taking place at the level of language or myth" (*DQ* 117). Ultimately the entire patriarchal tradition and its mode of reason is challenged by Don Quixote's quest including religious institutions (a Catholicism run by religious white men bearing the image of woman as the Virgin Mary), political institutions (President Reagan [101] and "greedy politicians" [68]), educational and marriage institutions, democratic ideals, and late-capitalist America ("VISA-ACCESS accounts" [182]). "I'm fighting all of your culture," cries Don Quixote (14). Referring to the masculine order of enchantment that defines our reality and puts us all (like dogs) at a state of war, Acker writes: "A white toga, which signifies the highest form of human culture knowledge and being-in-the-world in our Western history, is hanging off this hairy ape-flesh. Since reality/my seeing can't be clear, he's either eating a half-peeled banana and/or holding a cross" (*DQ* 75). The myth that we all live in a democratic or free world is probably the most unfair to the "dogs" in *Don Quixote* who like women in the culture at large, have always been denied equality in desire and language as well as at greater sociopolitical and institutional levels. Denied community, individuals are free to fight like dogs in "poverty, alienation, fear" (*DQ* 190) according to the capitalist code and to its inner workings of power.

Acker's exasperation is nothing short of a battle cry in a gender war [3] that kills women: "Doggish life depends upon unequal power relations or the struggle of power.... The condition of a dog is a condition of war against everyone.... This is freedom" (*DQ* 114). The offer of "freedom" in America is a "mask of death" (*DQ* 115). Women aren't free to love or be subjects (i.e., speak) and hold identities. A woman is dead in all of these ways because, as Acker writes, her access to language is suppressed since language is a masculine construct: "Being dead, Don Quixote could no longer speak. Being born into and part of a male world, she had no speech of her own. All she could do was read male texts which weren't hers" (*DQ* 39). All women are born dead (shackled) because they are forced to live out the masculine cultural text (the simulacra of late-capitalist phallocracy). On the other hand, Don Quixote dies in the novel because her pursuit of love and advocacy of female desire have brought her beyond the social order where she risks death (or insanity). Dix asserts:

> Don Quixote is on the edge of an abyss, for she realizes that her stance as a revolutionary has brought her to a place where she is trapped by her own desires to change reality into something better. This is the dangerous aspect of any line of flight: on one side rests the danger of being overcome by the state apparatus, and on the other side there is the possibility of "falling off the edge," where the nomad runs the risk of losing control of her becomings and consequently yields herself up to either the controls of others (by going "insane") or death. (60)

In the end, Don Quixote embraces her madness because it is necessary "to foray against the owners of this world" (*DQ* 193). As she releases her revolutionary dream and the (k)night falls (*DQ* 207), the ending suggests the impossibility of love, liberated desires, identity, happiness, or saving the world. Acker writes: "This world in which we are now living is crawling on its hands and knees through its muck without any desire to drill through the sky to reality" (*DQ* 193-194). Readers are left a last image of Don Quixote, in which the dogs of the world hold her bleeding flesh between their teeth (*DQ* 201), before they exit the novel and "aw[a]ke to the world that lie before [them]" (*DQ* 207). Any redeeming qualities are garnered from the fact that the novel has given us a language, like the dogs who sing at its conclusion, to interpret the reality that awaits us. The knight boldly states: "Language is community, Dogs, I'm now inventing a community for you and me" (*DQ* 191). This rebellious semantic site at the boundaries of culture (*DQ*), the (k)night's fight against the ideals, the myths, images and misrepresentations of the dominant structure, her refusal to conform to these conventions of the enchantment that transverse various political, historical, social, and aesthetic fields all serve to deconstruct that phallogocentric order.

Chapter Seven

Clarence Major's *My Amputations*: African American Identity and Simulacra

> The subject needs a myth of its end, as of its origin, to form its identity.
>
> —Jean Baudrillard, *Symbolic Exchange and Death*

Clarence Major's novel, *My Amputations*, illustrates in many respects the fatal nature of identity in a postmodern culture. Between its pages, African American identity is presented as a simulacrum of fractal components that overwhelm the main character, Mason Ellis, in his allegorical quest for identity (where simulacral living might be equated with a metaphoric death). The novel brings to light the problem of to what extent authenticity is possible in our contemporary world, where identity is always a series of masks, or simulacra. Like a postmodern onion skin, there is no true entity underneath the layers of masks, no authentic identity that is not always already a product of Western culture. Many masks are tried on during the main character's transcultural journey that surveys multifarious levels of identity. At each level, as each mask is discarded, an "amputation," or a "loss of self" occurs. That is, as Mason unveils himself of these masks that comprise his molar identity (media stereotypes, cinematic roles, and identity as Other—not only as a black man, but as a black author)—his identity is "transfigured" and remains "unfinished" (190). For Giles Deleuze and Felix Guattari, the molar individual is a bad copy of the model that exists as a whole (cultural image of unity to which it conforms) always in addition to its multiplicity, or molecular makeup (Massumi 54-55). bell hooks writes that "Postmodern critiques of essentialism which challenge notions of universality and static over-determined identity within mass culture and mass and consciousness can open up new possibilities for the construction of self and assertion of agency . . . . Such a critique allows us to affirm multiple black identities, various black experiences. It also challenges colonial imperialist paradigms of black identity which represent blackness one-dimensionally in ways that reinforce and sustain white supremacy" (qtd. in Pfohl 32).[1] This framework of identity (molar vs. molecular) leaves the body the option of becoming what it is said to be (a simulacrum) or a neurotic breakdown in the presence of so many unactualized potentials for "becoming"—and a possible breakaway to undifferentiated schizophrenia (Massumi 92).

The progression of the narrative in *My Amputations* depicts the main character's neurosis in simultaneously constructing and fragmenting an identity, symptomatic of the fractal nature of the postmodern subject. In *Baudrillard Live: Selected Interviews*, Jean Baudrillard remarks on our current state of affairs: "You certainly find this frantic search for identity, but its 'reality,' if I may use the term within quotation marks, is rather promiscuity, re-mixing and modes of interchange, that is to say, the great game of de-identification" (135). Henry Louis Gates's "Beyond the Culture Wars: Identities in Dialogue," reverberates these sentiments in discussing some of the limitations of multiculturalism and the paradoxes of liberal individualism. While recognizing the instability of the individual subject as a category, society tries to constitute cultural unities at the level of not only ethnicity, but gender and race under the rubric of multiculturalism as a whole. Gates cites the French anthropologist Jean-Loup Amselle's critique of multiculturalism, warning against the artifact of discreet ethnicity, in favor of multiplicity (8). Gates's point is exactly what Mason comes to find out is "real," that "identity politics cannot be understood as a politics in the harness of a pre-given identity" (9). *My Amputations* presents the fundamental problems when identity politics, which are concerned with the survival of an identity (Mason's search for the Name), come into conflict with a discourse of liberation (Mason's quest for an authentic identity apart from cultural representations).

As Gates points out, multiculturalism is concerned with representations of differences in cultural identities (6), but this results in alienation in the face of economic and social inequities because the dominant culture ideologically codes the "self" according to these markers of difference. For example, Mason is alienated by personifying the cultural stereotypes of the viral (porno movies), yet always absent, black Father (numerous children by different wives (13), and criminal (bank robber). Just like on TV, Mason's early life (before incarceration), is the perfect simulacrum of the "black male." There is a cynical element to the novel that depicts the flip side to the mythical character of individualism that is, in fact, co-opted under the sign of simulation culture. Here, along the postmodern terrain, "the 'self' has become a sign of itself, a double dramaturgical reflection anchored in media representations on the one side, and everyday life on the other" (Denzin viii). In the novel, Mason Ellis never succeeds at becoming anything more than the image of a famous black author ("Richard Wright") or stereotypical black male in contemporary TV culture. What is evident here is that "ethnic" difference isn't possible in commodified culture when difference (in the form of "identity") is always subsumed under the sign of the same.

How then, does one escape that simulacrum that continuously returns to confront us in our culture where gender and racial identities are always (re)produced? For Friedrich Nietzsche, it becomes an issue of the "will to power," of "becoming" among masks and finding "difference in the eternal return of the same." Most of us wear masks and discard them for new ones as we author our lives—life as an artistic creation that we might will the return of, again and again. The novel has a sense of return in its characters who all reappear and in the depiction of the circle. Mason is referred to as The Prodigal Son, and the narrator says "Something linear about this circle. . . ." of masks (204-205). As simulacra, things return through the same conceptual categories, images, and appearances, through a perceived time of linear difference. (Look at the wealth of movie sequels today, or consider the strings of "genre" movies that reference themselves through a montage of borrowed skits, lines, images, and parts recycled from other movies.) In Mason Ellis's journey back through a black-and-white ancestry, he realizes that there is no authentic cultural identity for him as a black author (militant, or political stereotypes), black American (welfare fraud [12]), or black man (criminal). There is no homogenous African-American identity found in the return, only reduplication of a Westernized past.

Mason eventually becomes imprisoned in the fiction (the novel, the circle of masks, and his "false past" [126]) and lost in simulacra he discovers his own genealogical quest for identity (for an authentic vs. counterfeit "self" in dialogue between Self and Cultural Other). As writer-searcher for a black "self" he is never able to escape the "white man's" domain, and spends his life "between the parenthesis" (175). Mason becomes enslaved by the recurrent simulacra (masks) he finds his identity layered in, which serve to situate him within normalized institutional, economic, and political constructs. When Achimota, the old poet who spoke of Langston Hughes, asked: "Are you a political poet?" Mason felt like "somebody was about to throw a ball for him to go and fetch" (182)—a repetitive motion of the same questions and postures he must repeatedly assume an identity from. Mason's attempts to "free" him/self ("freemason") from these snares by writing his way out (7) becomes a dangerous and slippery quest in which he risks losing his very being: "Perhaps the spirit of Arapahoe and hoodoo itself would protect this native son on the white slopes" (76), Major writes. The novel exemplifies the disappearance of Self in Culture—how having a stable identity is sublimating to the imprisonment of the social and the cinematic. Moreover, as such, Mason Ellis represents the heritage of the nihilistic subject doubled under the screenal sign of postmodernity and within the contours of Western culture that can only be "willed" past.

Mason's quasi-genealogical retracing of (His)tory through the imperialism of Western culture (America-Europe-Greece-Africa [126]) ends not in emancipation or the revelation of a primordial cultural authenticity, but in concession to a circle of "wooden masks" (204-205). The self-conscious plot of the novel carries him to Africa. While in Greece, he wonders: "If he were a product of the West—and this was the "cradle" of the West, then . . . well add two and two. Do You get Africa? (174). Still, Africa, itself the "cradle of humanity," was shocking (190). His driving into the Ivory Coast reveals a white imperialist commercialization and simulation which, ironically, marks the region as a product of the West as well. The narrator posits: "Mason felt as though he was in some modern European metropolis: massive traffic jams, skyscrapers, the whole bit" (191). There are no pure roots found here. In fact, at the village, Bopola-Ganori, where the final mask is put on, he is left with no "self" and his search for a mythical identity ends (in a metaphoric death). Mason's revelation as he completes the allegorical C of the circle of masks is that there are only masks (the myth of a unitary subjectivity dispelled), and he "come[s] to the end of [his] running" (205). The letter C and the numerous "curved" imagery of himself depict Mason throughout the text (148, 174, and 203). His family lived at "Apartment C" between Church Avenue and State Street (5); and he has lost faith in both Church and State (3). What readers discover in traveling through the text is that identity is always already doubled under the "parabolic" sign of Western, white, patriarchal culture, and that we are all (male, female, Asian, and black) imprisoned within its semiurgical effects that cannot be shed or transcended, only reproduced. Baudrillard comments on the hyperreal state of things once they lose "whatever served as cause, origin, referential, finality, etc.—into a form which multiplies itself effectively until it becomes fatal to itself . . . it finds a type of fatality in its own effects" (*BL* 84).

My Amputations brings to the forefront the problem of an autonomous subjectivity, of "free-becoming" in contemporary culture, of the impossibility at creating an authentic "self" in a culture in which the Zeitgeist is "resemblance" (*SIM* 142). In our postmodern universe reality itself has begun the fatal trajectory to resemble the image. In a nightclub in Monrovia, Mason sees previous characters out of context and in disguises. The novel depicts that progressive movement through the masks of identity (in the forms of resemblance—"they all look the same to me") that our culture provides for a black author and a black man to wear to assume identity. Mason Ellis (M/E) discovers the impossibility of an authenticity in postmodernity when he must impersonate or resemble the identity of the Author who is, according to Mason, the impostor of Mason himself. That is, the impostor, Clarence Mckay, has apparently stolen Mason's manuscript while he was in prison at Attica and become an acclaimed writer, creating an identity and Name that Mason Ellis must assume: "Mason had to deal with this shammer in the only way one deals with a conspirator: to outdo him he had to become a supreme impostor himself" (28). Public Enemy advises Mason to do away with the impostor and assume his rightful identity that has been affixed to his manuscript; "You got to *create* yo identity!" (28). Thus, Mason Ellis becomes the impostor. This excursion begins as Mason leaves the prison and enters culture, which is ironic because it is in his position as a black man in culture that he discovers the prison of simulacra that is identity in postmodernity. He is always marked in the form of a sign of cultural differentia ("Other") that maintains that position within the dominant culture and, hence, withholds assimilation, and from which he wished to "free" himself. Major writes: "Wasn't he really playing the ultimate pinball machine of luck and trying (even with a false name) to be himself . . . [a] true freemason?" (136). His transhistorical journey crosses the United States, (growing up on the streets of Chicago; facing the military's discrimination in Texas, Georgia, and Florida during the 1950s (33); and being imprisoned in New York) and eventually leads him to Europe (the Great Imperialists) and Greece (the foundations of writing, politics, and the State); but he is never able to escape the colonization of Western images.

As the novel progresses, it is more and more obvious that Mason will never establish a "Name," and he doubts "his ability to be himself" (162-163). At one point, the Narrator refers to Mason as "the King of Illusion-Deceit-Fraudulence-Cheating-Shenanigan[s]" (106). As impersonator-plagiarist he runs to "free" him/self and to create another "self." He is a fraud because he maintains this status within Western culture as he travels back through it (from Attica in the United States to Attica in Greece) and merely reduplicates his identity in the process. He is also revealed as a fraud when he signs the wrong name to the contract of the Magnan-Rockford Foundation (139). But in this act he begins to understand his predicament, "The signing of the contract? Hadn't he begun the long surrender of the Self? . . . He would go on, wouldn't he: vanishing and resurfacing alternately till he achieved his identity or disappeared forever" (155). This scene foreshadows the unraveling of the plot and the conclusion of the novel. It follows "then the dream cleared. He'd been trapped on a tribal set. Surrounded by strangers" (155). In the pages that follow, ironically, as Mason runs toward identity, he "cuts" off parts of his past until he comes to the end where he can't escape the surrender of the flesh to the image. This occurs symbolically when the final mask is put on and he completes "the circle of wearers of masks (205). The statement: "keep this nigger"

(204).... "You, my son, have come to the end of your running" (205) brings the narrative to closure, returning to the representations Mason's life began with amid the discrimination of the 1950s.

I would like now to turn to what might be called the autobiographical nature of the text and the manner by which it questions the author's relation to a literary past. In some ways, *My Amputations* presents the postmodern story of "becoming" an author and a "self," which means realizing the ultimate fragmentation and loss of both when identity is always-already created as a mask (identity-made commodity) for you to wear. Will Mason (or Major, for that matter) be able to "free" himself from the simulacra of a cultural past and forge a new identity as a authentic black author? It is impossible to escape the presence of the past that is everywhere occurring around us in simulation. Mason's identity is always already comprised by a reduplication of past literati, for example, Richard Wright's *Native Son* is repeatedly alluded to, as illustrated in this quote.

Although Mason attempts to free himself from the literary past and cultural images of black identity, because he is always forced to impersonate other black authors or to steal his identity from the Impostor, Mason's own authorial identity remains obscured by, or layered in, this constructed wall of masks. When he enters the bookstore, he cannot locate his "Name" among other American authors" (91). In Attica, he read a lot of other authors whom he would quote and imitate (Joseph Conrad, Herman Melville, and James Joyce) (40). In fact, throughout the novel, Mason, is continually confused with other black authors and celebrities and challenged concerning their political agendas. In London he's asked: "How could a Black poet write other than *anger*? . . . You nigger to the white man, like me" (105). At another of his readings: "they loved him already: he was early Dick Gregory, late Richard Pryor (63). When he tells one lecture hall audience about his writing "'I'm just beginning to find myself on my own. I want to speak to you about my new effort to re-create myself. . . .'" (59) they trivialize the attempt at purging his "self-betrayal" by asking: "'Did you write a book called *Native Son*? "No." "How about *Invisible Man*?" . . . "Do you know Toni Morrison?'" (59). His exasperation herein notwithstanding, the theme of identity-building resounds in his name "Mason" and the references to bricklaying in the text (176). The narrator poses: "And this deeper question (even halfway admitted to himself) of the scathed name, of forged identity, with its built-in layer upon layer of the genuine the unreal the sort-of-authentic" (115). And later, he thought to inscribe his name in stone, like Byron, at the Temple to Poseidon (176).

Mason Ellis's "search" (172) for authorial identity, his will to "place my x" (118) somewhere, develops along the lines of the detective novel he finds *him/self* in the writing of (99). His quest for identity will gather force from his ability to put together the "forced connections" between his novel and the novel by Clarence Major in which he is already a character (187-188). When he begins his "work in progress" he refers to it as if "his life depended on it. It was no longer just the blank page he had to face" (126). Mason Ellis (or M/E) starts to create him/self on page 64: "I am concerned with an encamped deeper sense of who I am, this character that is me." Later, in a dream where Mason had been "trapped on the tribal set," the man in the loin skin who examines his urine reports: "This man, rough, and in need of revisions, better focus, cutting, pasting, more action and less telling, is faced with a monumental decision. . . . My son, you are about to discover how to pull it all together" (156). He was first told to create himself in Attica, which is where he began to read other writers: "Was this the same Mason who in the joint had read the Author's works over and over again till he convinced himself he was the writer and no longer the reader" (40). This is also, supposedly, where his identity is lost to Mckay who steals and publishes his manuscript. From this passage, readers have to wonder whether or not Mason ever really authored the manuscript; regardless, he still searches to establish an identity for himself as a black author. There are numerous references to Mason's nebulous self-identity in the novel. In the kidnapper scene "he had to quickly do something aggressive or he'd lose not only what little identity he had left but his entire existence" (113). At a masquerade party he is called Mr. Nobody" (166). Again, here is another allusion to the *Invisible Man* where to be black is to essentially have no identity. Earlier in the novel, Mason announces: "I needn't tell you I'm not the Invisible Man: yet race—or its absence—remains part of my identity" (64).

Through the course of the novel, readers come to realize that the detective story Mason is writing is about recovering the "Author" (himself) from this palimpsest of impersonations, which as it gathers force, reveals itself coiled within the plot of the novel written by Major. That is, Mason's novel is about his pursuit of the Impostor depicted in the novel written by "C"larence Major. The narrator ponders: "If I tie a string to his nervous little finger and connect it to a large C hanging, say, in the sky, then connect the C to Celt [Mason's muse] and from her stretch it from myself to Mason, then jerk the end of the damn thing—what would happen? Would I get any added up, totalized meaning, plot?" (37). The narrator constantly bemuses the "forced connections" between Mason, McKay, and Major (187), and the plausibility of the plot line itself, until ultimately the "work in progress" written by Mason and the novel we are reading by Major merge: "One thing was clear though: [Mason] was not just drifting: the design was terrifying in its connections" (167). As Mason writes out his life, it becomes increasingly unclear as to where he is in the intersections, where he knows he must not get carried away (174). At one point, Mason dreams that he "was writing a novel in which he couldn't figure out the difference between what was real and not" (103). This is that novel that he is living. His "life depends" on delineating the "differences between real characters and fake people" (64). Mason's quest to escape this fictionalization he is experiencing is futile because he is all the time simulating the "real" notion of the Author.

In *Simulations*, Baudrillard says that in postmodernity, individuals substitute "the signs of the real for the real itself" (4). Mason participates in the process of simulation when he assumes the identity of Clarence Mckay. In the age of simulation, the image, the impersonator, can easily replace the real, because there is no difference. This is because the definition of the real becomes: "*that of which it is possible to give an equivalent reproduction*" (*SIM* 146). Throughout the novel, Mason replaces the black author with the signs of being a black author and no one recognizes the difference—except for a woman from Brooklyn College he had sex with, and this only because of his size: "You see, I know because I fucked the *real* dude: his cock is bigger" (italics mine, 70). This means of identification is itself no more than a trite reference to the black man's penis size. Even here at this moment of intimacy, where Mason might extract his real identity from its counterfeit "self," what is "real," the flesh, loses out again to the sign. Mason's odyssey never leaves the realm of appearances. Everywhere around us today what is real is being played out as appearances (*SIM* 12). The postmodern condition is the knowledge that "appearance" (or the image) has passed through the following successive phases from reflecting a basic reality, to masking a basic reality, to masking the *absence* of a basic reality, to bearing no relation to any reality whatever: it is its own pure simulacrum (*SIM* 11). Mason exemplifies this as he assumes the identity of the Author and begins to travel the circuit; and the identity he creates is inextricable from the simulacra (masks) he finds and the expectations he encounters being an African American writer.

Major accepts these simulacra as well when he writes and wears the masks of black authors, thus manifesting the signs of what it means to be a an African American author. He too, might be considered one who writes to "conceal" the tropic nature of his discourse and simultaneously exacerbate the autobiographical nature of his search in his fiction. Major writes: "Nietzsche was right on at least one point: writers wrote to conceal. The possible reality of the effort?" (116). Isn't this what all authors do, when they borrow words from language, ideas form experiences with others, plots from other narratives, and so forth. They represent the real; that is, to create, they are concealing the fact that they are filling in difference with the same, the real with fiction, absence with language—that they write from the same impulses of the nihilistic subject. In Lacanian discourse, the Real is that which language can never quite grasp.

Finally, this novel about a black writer trying to uncover his true identity leads us back to the question of the Author and the Name. The names are too similar to be dismissed as coincidence. First, Mason Ellis is conspicuously similar to Ralph Ellison, and many literary allusions to *The Invisible Man* are in evidence. Also the initials M/E that Mason brands on his chest indicate that readers should speculate as to whom this "M/E" is (58). Mason is as much an impostor as the Author (Clarence McKay) who "shadows" him from page 1 and whom he must impersonate, though he claims that he is the originator of the literature. Mason can never gain autonomous authority, since that M/E is always garnered from stolen parts. Mason cannot supplant or escape the Impostor, for it is he who is guilty. He struggles with this "stranger," or Impostor, which his identity has become when he looks in the mirror and cannot identify himself (82). Major writes: "This wasn't Mason Ellis . . . Mason himself was closer to the arc of a circle—slightly bent from despair and running. The mirror then might be the intersection of two sets" (82). This image of "running" recurs at the end of the novel when the Chief says "you, my son, have come to the end of your running" (205). Again, literary allusions abound, first with the wordplay on "son" that acknowledges a legacy to Richard Wright (*Native Son* 144) or Ralph Elli(son)'s *Invisible Man*. The ending, where Mason is to present the envelope to Chief Q. Tee, echoes the ending of that novel, as well. The intersection here, is the legacy of past and present masks (cultural, ethnic, and authorial) that converge at this moment in the novel, and may also indicate that both the Impostor, Clarence McKay, and the Impersonator, Mason Ellis, comprise Clarence Major. The novel, itself, questions the narcissistic mirroring of identity: "Mason's good intentions were not writerly, folks" (116)—he was trying to write himself "out from under" (116) the influences of these layers of masks. Mason's indebtedness to other black authors is obvious, and, clearly, Clarence Major experiences this same anxiety of influence. It is too conspicuous that the initials for Clarence Major and Clarence McKay (the Impostor) are the same. And the letter C is each one's, as well as Celt's (Mason's muse) first initial. At one point Mason is introduced as born in Chicago and the writer of an anthology of African-American Slang (62). Major was born in Chicago and is the author of a dictionary of African-American Slang—*Juba to Jive*. The plight of both men is the same postmodern predicament to have to steal your material when there is nothing new to be written or said. Readers might gather that Clarence Major is speaking of his own cultural borrowings from other black identities and voices (Claude McKay?), and that he perceives of his own voice as an inauthentic stand-in.

True to the hysteria characteristic of today: "the hysteria of production and reproduction of the real" (*SIM* 44), what we discover from Major's novel is the hyperreal author who in his life and writing can never escape the presence of the past and can only reproduce the story of what it means to be an author. Mason's identity and his writing are nothing but the return of simulacra—cultural past, a literary past, and media stereotypes—all the masks that confront him. Even Mason's "work in progress" turns out to be the same novel he is a character in already written by Major. Fredric Jameson claims that postmodern art will be art about itself in a new way whose "essential messages will involve the necessary failure of art and the aesthetic, the failure of the new, the imprisonment in the past" (115-116). Under the equivalency of the sign, life, like art, now confused with its image, will only be able to reduplicate its past and "to imitate dead styles, to speak through the masks and with the voices of the styles in a museum"

(115). This is to concede to the order of simulacra—where all reality is of the order of "that which is always already reproduced" (*SIM* 146). Like Masons's blank ambivalence upon entering the circle of masks at the end of the novel, like all of us who concede our identities to the designer lifestyles presented to us on televisions everyday, art enters into its indefinite reproduction. That is, in the same manner that Mason's identity stays confined within layers of representation and our(selves) subject to the hyperaesthetization of everyday living, neither is the work of art emancipated from this realm of "being."

Is there line of flight here from the striated social sphere to smooth space of open-ended identity? Mason Ellis never really escapes a molar vector of prefigured identities to a supermolecular "becoming-other." He merely reaches a fatal state of equilibrium in "becoming" the prefabricated or canned version of personhood societal representations offer him ("sameness"). On the other hand, do we find (dis)simulation within the simulacra? Only if it might serve as a hyperaesthetic exposure of the image-mongering system of power that authorizes certain representations and invalidates others. In this light, Major's work goes beyond parody to the blankness of pastiche. As Mason is about to enter the circle of masks, he questions its seriousness: "Pastiche"? (205). Major's "amputated" and fragmented text reads as a testimony to the hyperreal loss of meaning to equivalences and play of reproduction. In this sense, *My Amputations* makes what Baudrillard describes as a "passage to a space whose curvature is no longer that of the real, nor of truth, the age of simulation thus begins with a liquidation of all referentials—worse: by their artificial resurrection in systems of signs, a more ductile material than meaning, in that it lends itself to all systems of equivalence" (*SIM* 4). Equivalence occurs in blank parody when reality is confused with its own image, as in the novel's conclusion, where all meaning is leveled to the order of masks.

Chapter Eight

Baudrillard's *America*: The Perfect Postmodern Object of Simulation

> American "being" in the postmodern condition: waiting with no expectation of real relief from the detritus of simulacrum; communication as radical isolation; endless motion as the nervous system of the culture of style, radical dislocation as the inevitable end-product of shifts in neo-technical capitalism.
>
> —Arthur Kroker, *The Postmodern Scene*

Reminiscent of Umberto Eco's *Travels in Hyperreality*,[1] Jean Baudrillard's book *America* is a travelogue through a culture fascinated with its own emptiness. Baudrillard sees America as a society that thrives on the obscenity of the image, the hyperreal, and simulation. He believes Americans are "themselves simulation in its most developed state" (*America* 28-29). Real culture is alien to America: "it is Disneyland that is authentic here! The cinema and TV are America's reality! The freeways, the Safeways, the skylines, speed, and deserts—these are America, not galleries, churches, and culture" (*America* 104). Because it has no supposed history of its own, America has been forced to create one. Hollywood, as a center of simulation, is the primary place where America manufactures for itself an "astral," or "orbital" sense of history and culture through the screenal succession of signs, images, and surfaces. Moreover, Baudrillard observes that "even outside the movie theater the whole country is cinematic. The desert you pass through is like a set of a Western, the city a screen of signs and formulas" (*America* 56). Evolving as a cinematic society, what some might consider America's own (once) genuine history—America's western frontier—has been transformed into a simulacrum (e.g., spaghetti Westerns). Baudrillard remarks that "The cinema has absorbed everything—Indians, *mesas*, canyons, skies" (*America* 69). And the metropolis offers the same "desert-like banality" of "televisual scenery" (*America* 9). For a more contemporary example of how reality disappears into the mediascape, take the Gulf War, when the (hyperreal) event seemed to take place exclusively on TV, even to those who were there, according to Baudrillard. [2] Consider the simulacral nature, or TV-mediated character, of the war—complete with ratings battles between the networks and CNN and commercial competition—that preempted the reality of the conflict (death, devastation, etc.). In similar fashion, Disney wants to build its newest theme park, "Colonial Disney," on top of *real* Civil War battlegrounds in Virginia. This truly is the site where reality is effaced by simulation. At Disney, as in America in general, reality is always inferior to imitation.

Baudrillard has stated that Disneyland creates for us the comforting, yet mythical, belief that the simulacra on its outside represents the "real." In "Simulacra and Simulations," in *Selected Writings*, Baudrillard says that Disneyland conceals the fact that "real" America is by nature Disneyesque. That is, "Disneyland is presented as imaginary in order to make us believe that the rest is real, when in fact all of Los Angeles and the America surrounding it are no longer real, but of the order of the hyperreal and simulation" (172). From this vantage point, Disneyland, like Las Vegas or MGM, serve as microcosms of America and of the Western world (*America* 55): the fact that these places are all totally emptied of all reality serves precisely *as* their (hyper)reality. In this "artificial paradise" (*America* 8), bolstered by a belief in the power of simulation, the ecstatic form of utopia is achieved (*America* 97). Or is it the simulation of utopia ("anti-utopia?")—finally epitomized in Reagan, who was never anything more than the performer, or the advertising image that doubled as a sign of power (*America* 108)—that is realized within a purely artificial society of appearances without depth, leaving to America the destiny of indifference, or the nonending evaporation and "desertification" of meaning (*America* 5)? In this light, one might see America as "[t]he desert of the real itself (*SIM* 2). Certainly one can perceive of America, which is home to the Miss America and Miss USA pageants, as the land of appearances. In these TV-spectacles the "master of appearing beautiful" wins it all—the trips around the world, the modeling contracts, a lifetime supply of shampoo, and so forth. And there isn't a woman in America who doesn't, to some degree, feel the futile pressure to participate in this "pageantry" on a daily basis! In the beauty pageant of consumer culture, patriarchal society serves as the judge and the male-driven advertising industry passes out sentences with the images it creates for women to live up to (and live out), or face rejection, castigation, and loss of self-esteem at the very least, and everything from mental depression to self-inflicted physical harm at the extremes. In America, the land of freedom, seduction, or the play of appearances, is the only option offered.

Cautioning us on page 1 that "*[o]bjects in mirror may be closer than they appear,*" Baudrillard reads America as representative of the life that lies in store for everyone who follows the simulation industries on a journey that leads to an insignificant "point of no return" (*America* 10). He poses the question in the first chapter, "Vanishing Point," of "how far can we go in the extermination of meaning, how far can we go in the non-referential desert form without cracking up and, of course, still keep the esoteric charm of disappearance?" (*America* 10). The desert is a site where human signs disappear, leaving only the indifference of pure objects, neutrality, and dead images that characterize contemporary America. Baudrillard sees America similarly approaching this "vanishing point" of the social, meaning, truth, history, the real (*America* 10). In Andrew Ross's view of Baudrillard, even the social has been horizontalized like the desert: "reduced to a flat, screenlike surface which simulates a sense of occasion without depth, affect, or history" (215). In an interview with J. Henric and G. Scarpetta, Baudrillard comments on his use of the motif of the desert in *America*: "[I]t's a kind of sidereal location. In such a place one lets oneself drift freely while still retaining—even at its most extreme limits—a sense of simulation" (*BL* 132). Why is the desert fascinating, Baudrillard asks in *America*? "It is because you are delivered from all depth there—a brilliant, superficial neutrality, a challenge to meaning and profundity, a challenge to nature and culture, an outer hyperspace, with no origin, no reference-points" (124). Indifferent and without depth, America is "[d]esert for ever."

Emptied of desire and free of seduction (hence, similar to the desert), the American culture is described by Baudrillard as a "*degree zero,*" where total absence equals pure presence (*America* 124). Like the postmodern sign, the infinite simulation of absence in the desert serves as an immanently reversible presence. Keeping in kind with his belief about the hyperreal nature of America, the disappearance of difference into empty images and meaningless representations of itself is the fatal strategy of our culture: "Nowhere else does there exist such a stunning fusion of a radical lack of culture and natural beauty, of the wonder of nature and the absolute simulacrum" (*America* 126). The desert, hence, is the emblem of America, since everywhere you look in either you find the sign of itself replicated over and over. (Consider any fast-food or convenience store chain, or subdivision, for that matter). According to Ross, the desert offers "extreme deliverance from lived social space, temporality and desire. This desert is obscene and fascinating because it has eliminated every possible means of seduction" (222).

Whereas, for Baudrillard, Europe is rich in aesthetic meaning (hence seduction), America is vastly superficial and displays an obscene one-dimensionality of signs; it is like a desert, emptied of aesthetic meaning (*America* 124). Lacking seduction (*America* 7), everything is made available and pornographic in America—talk shows and news show exposés, such as *A Current Affair*, saturate the networks. Every event that takes place seems of value only if it makes tabloid news. Like in Thomas Pynchon's *Vineland*, or Don DeLillo's *White Noise*, the TV-flow between real-life and video representation make the value of their separation nearly indiscernible. Because of the "hypervisibilty of the pornographic image and its corresponding loss of scene . . . the real can only be a continuation of representation" (Ross 224). America is only virtually real: "a society which constantly views itself reflected back to itself on the glare of the TV screen" (Denzin 140). The goal of everything now is to be hooked up to itself: "Without this circular hook-up, without this brief, instantaneous network that a brain, an object, an event, or a discourse create by being hooked up to themselves, without this perpetual video, nothing has any meaning today" (*America* 37). Look to the fashion and advertising industries where you are the image of yourself imagined on TV. All of America operates by the logic of the video loop hologram, which is like "a three-dimensional dream . . . you can enter . . . as you would a dream. Everything depends on the existence of the ray of light bearing the objects. If it is interrupted, all the effects are dispersed, and reality along with it" (*America* 30). Everything appears in the postmodern light as the most unreal of substances—a perpetual reduplication and simulation of itself. In this developed state of simulation, America lives a perpetual presen(t)ce as the model for itself (*America* 29): "Americans may have become reflections of the reflections that have been brought to them by the media-oriented, postmodern cinematic society" (Denzin 145). While, *The Brady Bunch Movie* leads box office sales, and on E! a documentary style program airs entitled *The Brady Bunch Chronicles: Portrait of an American Family*, complete with commentary from "real" historians, sociologists, and psychologists. (The same tactic was recently used with the entirely fictional *Blair Witch Project*.) Here we are presented with the hyperreality of a TV history willed by us to replace the real history of the 1970s (and why not?). As viewers wax nostalgic and posit their families as reflections (simulacra) of *The Brady Bunch* referent, reality is replaced with the emptiness of a TV representation.

Baudrillard concludes *America* with the same perceptions he carries throughout his journey—that America displays a primitive cultural desert like aura. He asserts that "This country is naive, so you have to be naive. Everything here still bears the marks of a primitive society: technologies, the media, total simulation (bio-, socio-, stereo-, and video-) are developing in a wild state in their original state. Insignificance exists on a grand scale and the desert remains the primal scene" (*America* 63). Baudrillard calls America a "primitive culture" because it lacks a rich historical or cultural past in which to root itself, and from which to reflect upon the present moment (*America* 7). In its totally primitive state, America replaces a sense of history or culture with the hyperreality of perpetual simulation. The speed at which history and culture are manufactured by the simulation industries in America, like the speed with which (vacant) signs of the desert reduplicate themselves before Baudrillard as he travels across it, leaves us without reference point or origin, so that we experience a cancellation of difference and an implosion of a sense of history. Baudrillard comments that "Speed creates pure objects. It is itself a pure object, since it cancels out the ground and territorial references-points, since it runs ahead of time to annul time itself" (*America* 6). Just drive down the strip at Daytona and lose perception of your place and time, where the scenery seems to reproduce itself continually, mile after mile after mile. Or find quintessential America in any McDonald's, in any city across the country, giving us a common means toward the inability to differentiate ourselves. Finally, experience the vertigo of comparing the two World Trade Center towers, which for Baudrillard signify the "end of every original reference" (*SE&D* 69). The fact that the towers double each other signals both the end of the original and the end of representation (because one can no longer distinguish between the two), just like the multiple replica faces of Marilyn Monroe on the famous Andy Warhol work (*SE&D* 70). At these fully American monuments to postmodernity, representation is effaced by reproducibility, duplication, and a simulation that achieves the total cancellation of differences and threatens to eradicate the very possibilities for meaning.

Chapter Nine

Media Culture on the Verge of Drama: Hyperreal O.J. and Simulacra in Oliver Stone's *Natural Born Killers*

> American society is not a society of appearances; it has no counterpart to the games of seduction.... The simulacrum is another game; its signs don't refer to any sense, they flow continually without reference to any sense.
>
> —Jean Baudrillard, *Baudrillard Live*

Commenting on the weakening vital signs of art in the American culture of mass media consumerism, Larry McCaffery states in the introduction to his book: *After Yesterday's Crash: The Avant-Pop Anthology*, that the landscape of pop-culture

> has increasingly become less a literal territory than a multidimensional *hyperreality* of television lands, media "jungles," and information "highways," a place where the real is now a "desert" that is "rained on" by a ceaseless "downpour" of information and data; "flooded" by a "torrent" of disposable consumer goods, narratives, images, ads, signs, and electronically generated stimuli; and peopled by media figures whose lives and stories seem at once more vivid, more familiar, and more real than anything an artist might create. (xiv)

Daily, it seems we witness the "desertification" of the real and its transformation into varying forms of "hyperreal" electronic, media, and TV representations. A strange phenomenon takes place at the sidereal location of television. There, reality is delivered from all depth, all meaning, and all origin outside of the references to television itself. In this process the media event is commodified and coded with all of the signifiers of the entertainment industry, the effect of which can be measured in the Gulf War that appeared as the greatest of miniseries, captivating more persons than *Roots* and leading to withdrawal and depression for many of us in our consumer culture, until finally it was packaged and re-sold in so many videocassette versions, collector trading cards, clothing lines, etc. Indeed, the distance between reality and its representations seems to have totally vanished into this hyperreal realm of televisual dramatization. Consider both the media sensationalism of the O. J. Simpson trial choreographed by the tabloid news programs associated with it, or the movie, *Natural Born Killers*, in which this TV-drama effect is made hyperbolic in the sitcom portrayal of Mallory's domestic life and the tabloid-style "documentary" of the killers that follows.

The precarious relationship between real and TV-representation has long since undergone a radical reversal, however. So many persons reference their "real" human experiences to episodes of shows like *The Brady Bunch* or model their behavior and language off of TV. For example, think of the retro-fifties style sideburns that made a resurgence after the airing of *Beverly Hills 90210*. Moreover, it seems as if now the real happens always already to be referenced to its hyperreal representation on television. With its corresponding loss of context as a televised image, the real readily becomes a continuation of a previously existing "scene" of television representations already familiar to us. A recent hurricane was noted by one national weather forecaster as being less like *Gone With the Wind* and more like *Waterworld*. In everything from HBO's *Real Sex* to the exposé coverage of *A Current Affair* and now the "O. J. Trial" on E! "real life" succumbs to its destiny to become the cinematic image, where real events occur to appear on TV, and it seems that no reality escapes the entertainment value that it must conform to.

The evidence that television explicitly recognizes its own self-referentiality is clear and present. During the O. J. Simpson trial there were constant indications of just this point: Down the streets from Universal Studios, at the Municipal Center for the City of Los Angeles, at high noon on June 30, 1994, as the proceedings of the pretrial for O. J. Simpson began the media specialist said something of this nature: "It's ironic that on the twenty-fifth anniversary of the Manson murders, Los Angeles, the city of cinema, produces yet another gruesome spectacle." On another channel, the CNN opening looked suspiciously like the opening of *A Current Affair*—O.J.'s picture gathered shape at the side of the screen and fit into place beside "The O. J. Simpson Trial." But what could be more perfect than a fractal O.J. whose media image had been shattered so that viewers might religiously watch it reconstructed, day by day, as a consumer spectacle for us to feed upon garnished with an array of commentary, advertisements, and other media images? Not since "The Gulf War" had daytime TV garnered such a viewing audience. Not even "The Menendez Brothers Trial," "The John Wayne Bobbit Story," or "The Nancy and Tanya Drama" carried such fine ratings. Just like on *Court TV*, Jack Ford came on to give expert analysis. Just like an episode of *Matlock*, a celebrity was arraigned for us to watch the mystery unraveled in true "cliff hanger" suspense. Just like the "WACO Incident," the "O. J. Simpson Story" would undoubtedly be ready for release, with all of the possible scenarios played out, well before the trial was over. And just like in a real Hollywood-produced movie, the forensics report was interrupted by flashbacks to June 13 depicting the gathering of evidence.

Similar to *JFK*, the details were formulated, the scientific evidence gathered, the medical studies produced, the interpretations mounted. Robert Shapiro interrogated: "When will the DNA test be administered; what manner of procedures; by whose qualifications?" Infinite truths, infinite perspectives were to be provided. In "Hyperreal O.J.," truth lay somewhere amongst—inseparable from—these representations. It seemed hauntingly like astral Waco where, in Texas, we found the perfect information overload, and verisimilitude assumed the appearance—in infinite parallel media universes—of a reality that unfolded as a made for TV movie, only to return again as "The Amy Fisher Story" and, this time round, as "Hyperreal O.J."

Over on CBS, the *New York Times* columnist Bob Herbert interjected that the entertainment value was being lost in the tedium, which translated into: "we may be losing viewers to *Montel*" (who was running a segment on "Twins Who Fight for Men's Sexual Attention" on another network). He went on to discuss with Dan Rather how the event was dramatized: "It won't be like *Perry Mason* and be tightly wrapped up in a thirty-minute episode." Rather raised the issue of whether O.J. would be allowed to sign football cards in his jail cell to gather money for his defense fund. A college fund for Simpson's children, to which viewers could contribute, might be set up. Under further speculation, would "1-900-SAVESOJ" allow us to cast our vote for whether or not he is innocent and "1-900-GOJUICE" give updated information on the case as it comes to light? Would there be any component free from commodification?

After a commercial break, NBC's opening juxtaposed the text "The People of California Against O.J." with an image of the famous #32 running back breaking tackles. A Warner Brothers logo flashed on the screen. It was the break between prosecution and defense questioning of Ms. Kessler—first Christopher Buckley commented, then syndicated columnist, then Mary Matalin, then Jack Ford again. An NBC court specialist said that Robert Shapiro might try to undermine the credibility of Ms. Kessler. As hyperinertia set in, where would astral O.J. come to rest among the testimonies, the evidence, the televisual images? Viewers were whisked off again to the Simpson estate, where at that moment investigators gathered further evidence. Brian Williams, the NBC reporter outside the courthouse, said: "The atmosphere is circuslike. Many people carry signs that say Free O.J. while others watch the trial inside on hand-held TVs."

Following another commercial break—*NBC Nightly News* with Tom Brokaw; Lense Crafters, Centrum, and *Frazier*—Brokaw returned to say that highlights from Wimbledon will be carried later. Forget Wimbledon; forget the World Cup; this was the biggest sports ticket ever. Back to live coverage the signs outside the courthouse said Free O.J.—from what? From the image, of course. Here was a man who, in his choreographed flee from defenders, was about to sacrifice the flesh (suicide) so that the image might live. Recall the image on that Friday night of O.J. on the run, pursued not only by the LAPD but by waves of fans cheering for their star to break free from his would-be interceptors? "Save the Juice," the fans roared. As his evasion of the law continued on the screen, fans held placards inscribed with Go! O.J. Go!, as if they were at a sporting event in a Buffalo stadium where "The Juice" was evading tackles, or, better yet, at a screening of his latest fast-action movie where he was to appear as an amphibious hero. What entertainment value! But haven't we seen *The Chase* before, only last time around it starred Charlie Sheen?

Two hours into the coverage, Tom Brokaw commented on the "real" O.J.: the Golden Boy of college football, the former Heisman Trophy Winner, the ESPN Sports commentator. By now it should be clear that on that Friday night O.J. ran to give us a parade of TV images to follow because he knew his flesh had been supplanted by the image. Like Bo Jackson, and Michael Jordan too, O.J. knows all too well that the image always replaces reality. Not only might the "real" O.J. (which he spoke of in his suicide letter), be the spectral *Monday Night Football* star, and the respected TV announcer, but, just as "real" is the knife-wielding fugitive or *A Current Affair* representation that appears everywhere in the media (the "lost person" capable of such heinous crimes). Why flee? There is no escaping; there is only the procession of dramatic images that must continue.

Live coverage shifted back to the O. J. Simpson's estate in Brentwood, where the search for evidence proceeded. Yet another commercial break followed with: MCI, Ex-Lax, *Baby's Day Out*, and Lens Crafters. For now, "Hyperreal O.J." was "To Be Cont'd...." Why, what else could come—a mystery novel canine with bloody paws leading to the scene of the crime or a secret envelope to be opened on Pay-Per-View? Or how about, "The O. J. Saga" trading cards, complete with pictures of the kids, Al Cowlings, and the "chase scene," or, better yet, a $19.99 videocassette of the chase scene itself? Two University of Alabama law students have since marketed a board game in which players move white Ford broncos around to determine the guilt or innocence of O.J., and win by proving it the predetermined way (established by a roll of the dice at the start of the game). And why not? Everyone who was watching the (hyper)real trial knew that guilt or innocence was no longer "really" the question because it was no longer ascertainable; there were too many distractions. The defense was now made up of infinite theories, studies, and calculations extraneous to the murders themselves. In the name of entertainment value, scenarios were played out, and "scripted" witnesses performed (e.g,. Detective Fuhrman—the prosecutions even told Fuhrman to watch *Rivera Live* to see if he recognized another witness). Geraldo Rivera did an entire show with a bowl of melting ice cream on his desk to test if a timeline theory fit.

In the meantime the courtroom drama miniseries kept running; it still garnered the top fifteen time-slot Nielsen ratings that week. David Lettermen joked that the ratings might be slipping, but urged us to have no fear, Ted Danson from *Cheers* would come on to play the bartender's role in the testimony. This totally media-made, TV-trial was now "about" being the biggest TV-spectacle ever, "about" being the "marking" event of the latter twentieth century. A newspaper cartoon at the time showed a woman watching the OJ trial on TV while she watched the soap opera *As the World Turns*, in which the characters were watching the O. J. Simpson trial. No one can escape the layers of "soap opera" hyperrealities outside of the TV as it seems to overflow into real life on a daily basis. On went the incessant flow of signs, images, and codes of the dominant consumer ideology and the entertainment industry that feeds it. Defense witnesses appeared and disappeared; many experts speculated that Miss Bell (in her fifteen minutes of fame) was attempting to get a line on her acting résumé with her accusations that Mark Fuhrman was a racist. "This is Hollywood," said a California judge on *Rivera Live*. That week's saga headliner, Brian "Kato" Kaelin would soon star in a movie presently being filmed. The TV transformation of the groundskeeper-made-celebrity came complete with daily makeovers, hairstyling, publicity coordinators, agents, talk shows, and now movie contracts. A news flash on E! said that Rodney King would be directing and starring in a movie soon to begin filming. On March 16, 1995, Judge Ito began the day by wishing a happy birthday to a friend in the viewing audience. Why not? The entire courtroom had been turned into a TV studio, and the trial participants seemed like actors and actresses complete with a Hollywood script far too impossible to have ever been anything other. By mid-April, the headlines read: "Marcia Clark's hairdresser will act as guest commentator."

On April 19, 1995 a news flash: "Oklahoma Explosion" tonight at 11:00. A special *Nightline* aired on ABC, *48 Hours* on CBS. This tragedy, not nearly complete at the time, had already begun to be served up to the public in commodity fashion. In the special coverage on CNN that evening, the OKLAHOMA CITY BOMBING logo flashed on between other commercials, complete with theme song introduction. And why not? All events are now made to conform to the image (always) already seen on TV and are destined to return for our consumption. The Monday following the terrorist bombing Oprah Winfrey broadcast a live show on the Oklahoma tragedy, complete with wide-screen TV coverage by a correspondent on the scene and interviews with loved ones of the missing. A computer simulated the bombing, making it all the more *real*. While during the commercial, on another network the gathering of evidence by Andrea Mazzola, LAPD specialist and Dr. Fung's assistant, was forced to conform to the scrutiny of videotapes that recorded her at the crime scene. And jurors watched the five minute laser disk video of the "enacted" drive from Rockingham to the Simpson estate on Bundy Drive—complete with digital timing and a simulated graphic mapping display. Not a moment of these totally hyperreal events escaped processing through the screenal image to confirm what *really* happened. In this case, reality appeared to us via a network of screens within screens.

O.J.'s lawyers yawned during the prosecution's presentation of DNA evidence on May 2, 1995, as if to say, it's too scientific, too factual, and precise to be of any value to this simulacral trial—viewers want only matters of speculation and conjecture to work with. On August 16, 1995: "This is a bombshell," exclaimed the defense attorney Johnny Cochran concerning the issue of the audiotapes of Mark Fuhrman making racial and sexist slurs. But what better thing than the tapes from a screenwriter's interview made some decade ago to push this trial over the edge of the postmodern abyss? Does it matter the context in which the tapes (the images, and the meanings) were created? All along this was always already a made-for-TV-event. "O.J." officially became a corporate commodity on September 19, 1995 when Simpson filed suit to have his name copyrighted as a logo because of all the commercialization surrounding the trial (the TV shows, products, etc.).

Finally, on September 26, 1995, closing arguments began. At the first commercial break of CNN's live coverage, new programming was announced: *Burden of Proof* would begin airing once the trial came to a close, starring former attorneys seen on the other talk shows, and a special guest—none other but Cochran himself. How perfect, "Hyperreal O.J." had spun off into another TV-world commodity so that our fetishized consumption of the image could continue. Then, at approximately 5:00 P.M., Judge Ito floored the world by apparently canceling the O.J. Trial series right at its climax, by turning off the camera. The media's attorney was right there though to save the day—probably threatening him with a lawsuit by a conglomerate of all of the major networks. On September 29, Marsha Clark concluded her rebuttal with the cinematic montage of audiovisual images! Finally, the result of the Microsoft poll on *Rivera Live* showed that 65 per cent of Americans polled found O.J. Simpson guilty and 35 per cent innocent. Yet, lest we forgot, the verdict of the "real" jury was still out. Then, the first advertisement ran for the three part videocassette "Murder Trial of O.J. Simpson," and the commodification spun onward.

On October 3, 1995, at 1:00 P.M., when the verdict of the O.J. Simpson trial was read on TV, the hyperreal atmosphere depicted a sporting event.

During the "pregame' coverage it was announced that the California Senate Affairs Committee had postponed speeches. Tom Brokaw anchored the "countdown," like the liftoff of the first space shuttle flight, while outside Rockefeller Center, a digital banner ran, and the crowd waved and cheered for the cameras that panned in on them. Brokaw heightened the drama with an allusion to the football heroics of O.J. saving the game in the last minutes on many occasions. Brokaw tried to go to the NBC superchannel in London to show the crowds watching at the pubs—to validify that this news event carried as much world attention as its counterpart in spectator violence—the Super Bowl. Switching instead to the crowd outside the Los Angeles Courthouse, it was noted that the presence of so many news helicopters made it feel like the filming to the sequel of *Apocalypse Now*—which was not a far reach from what the LAPD feared might occur if O.J. was convicted. With only a minute to go before "kickoff," Jerry Spence, Ira Reiner, Jack Ford, and Ray Black all appeared in a quarter of the screen to give us their last-minute predictions. The "books" were sealed with the final odds—*USA Today* had them listed at 2-1 "guilty." Someone on the panel of experts mentioned the defense team's Johnny Cochran had an undefeated record against the LAPD and that the prosecution team's Chris Darden had a winning streak of nineteen cases in a row. After the verdict was read, in NFL postgame fashion, the winning (defense) team was interviewed first with the loser (prosecution) to follow. Like many of the recent Super Bowls—this super spectacle was a blowout win for the "dream team"—only four hours of deliberation. The consumer spectacle of the century came to closure with a seemingly repeat performance of the Bronco chase—when helicopters followed the white van carrying O.J. through the interstate highways of Los Angeles for a final moment of heightened drama that lasted some twenty minutes or more. Finally, a juror Tracy Hampton posed for the March 1996 issue of *Playboy*, and it was revealed that the magazine had been offered an exclusive interview from O.J. for a measly $500,000 that it turned down. You can buy your personalized video of the "real" story today for $29.95 by dialing 1-800-O.J. Tells.

During the same time that this "real life" drama of the O.J. Simpson trial competed for a viewing audience with daytime TV soap operas, on the big screen, Oliver Stone's satire of America held nothing back in its efforts to bring us face to face with the "pornography" of ritualized sex and violence many of us have come to call "entertainment." In *Natural Born Killers*, Stone offers a veritable cornucopia of iconoclastic imagery so as to shatter the (hyper)reality immanent to the televisual or screenal imaging of our culture. More and more, in the obscenity of today's info-culture, private events enter the realm of the viewing audience. For example, picture Mallory, in *Natural Born Killers*, who is shown in a psychologically, sexually, and physically abusive relationship with her father—succulent subject matter for Montel or Jerry Springer. The only question for these programs is of the advertisers: "Will it sell?"

Mallory's adolescent history is presented to us through the perspective of a sitcom audience, complete with voice-overs, ads, and credits. The abusive childhoods of Mickey and Mallory apparently lead to their antisocial, pathological behavior and the killing spree that the audience participates in for the duration of the movie. This genre of "sex and violence" entertainment that viewers witness in *Natural Born Killers* is of the same kind that they feed upon from daytime talk shows, nightly news, and in the movies seen on cable TV. Thus, a hint of sarcasm is sent to the audience members themselves, most strongly felt in the statement by Wayne Gale that "Repetition works! Do you think those nitwits in zombie-land remember anything?" and at the movie's end when Wayne is killed and Mickey says: "I am killing you and what you represent"—a seemingly ironic act after referring to the unholy three-way marriage between the media, violence, and its viewers that he, in part, manifests.

Ultimately, Stone surpasses any simple moralizing concerning the regard our society holds for human life, to questioning any grounds whatsoever there might be for calling something "really" human in this day and age of simulacra—where it appears everywhere around us that real life happens as if to be on TV. For example, human tragedies (which are those events that "sell" best) seem to occur for the pleasure of the viewing audience (i.e., the consumer). How many people tune in nightly to see the rape and murders on the "real" news shows that are replayed later on the evening movie that follows (e.g., "The Menendez Trial," "The Tanya and Nancy Episode," "The Amy Fisher Story," or John Wayne Bobbit in porn movies)? The same sorts of stories that made celebrities out of these persons on the tabloid news shows correlate with the Mickey and Mallory sensationalism on the tabloid news program *American Maniacs* that transforms them into the sort of hero/icons that would induce the statement from one of the youth interviewed that "If I was going to be a mass murderer, I would be like Mickey and Mallory," or would cause fans to hold placards that read Go O.J. as he fled from the police on a California highway preempting the other regularly scheduled prime-time sporting event—the NBA playoffs—that unforgettable Friday night. If all the world's a stage, and we are merely players, today it seems ever more the case that the world has become a TV screen, and we are actors who perform to a script written for the profit of the networks—and more astoundingly, whose lives occur to return to us for our own viewing pleasure (see *Donahue, Montel, America's Funniest Home Videos,* or *The Real World*).

In this light, *Natural Born Killers* reveals a value system turned topsy-turvy by the hyperreality of television. The viewing audience worships the TV image so religiously that they equivocate it with fame. (How else could the groundskeeper turned movie star Kato Kaelin appear on the cover of *GQ*?). TV images are so often related to sex and violence that those persons associated with these images (Mickey and Mallory, Kato Kaelin, Amy Fisher, John Wayne Bobbit, and Charles Manson) become famous by default, regardless of any scepter of reality, immoral or otherwise, which might have shadowed those images. That "reality" has long since disappeared behind its representations in the media, cinema, and TV. How else could the Rodney King video verdict have been different in the two courts had the "reality" of violence not been lost to its hyperreal representations in shows such as *Cops*, CNN's Gulf War miniseries, and the nightly news broadcast? Recall the ever so familiar arrest scene at the Rx in *Natural Born Killers*.

As another contemporary example of how reality disappears into the mediascape, take the Gulf War—a simulacral event that seemed to take place exclusively on a TV-monitor, even to whose who were there. U.S. soldiers in their barracks in Saudi Arabia watched live TV coverage to follow the war, and, more astoundingly, Sadam Hussein's major flow of information came from CNN. Even the fighter pilots fired virtual missiles on video screens without ever seeing the "real" enemy. Consider the TV-mediated character of this hyperreal war—complete with ratings battles between the networks and CNN and commercial competition that preempted the reality of the conflict (fighting, death, devastation, etc.).

The present value system is established by the "entertainment value" that these simulacral events hold for us. This is why the O. J. Simpson trial so easily replaced the Gulf War as the biggest prime time ad spot, winning out over all of the other daytime soap operas. Would the trial have led the Nielsen Ratings for sixteen weeks if he weren't a superstar? During CNBC's late night talk show coverage of the O. J. Simpson trial, *Serial Killers* is offered for our video library. The sanctity of life and death, morality, and humanity are all superfluous matters. The hyperreality of the entertainment image as commodity seems to be all that matters. Look at any advertisement that offers the images of "success," "wealth," "beauty," or "youth'—just buy the associated product and the image is our reality. But can a Lexus car really offer power, Revlon beauty, or Pepsi youth? Nietzsche said in an age of nihilism (when, today, designer clothing instills in us a sense of our identities, we garner our lifestyles from the car we drive, and advertising narratives invoke in us romance) that individuals would have to find new forms within the recurring same representations to continue to "self-create," or simply exist.

Yet, this is nothing new. We have long been awash in an incessant flow of images that the media-centered culture now accepts as totally natural. The killing spree odyssey followed in *Natural Born Killers* is presented via a cinematic montage of 35-mm film, video, black-and-white footage, and animation that makes the murderous adventure appear all the more familiar, hence "real" to us. The effect is more accurately attributed to the hyperreal sensation of experiencing these same events where we always "really" do—on our TV screens. It is nothing for us to witness "real" death on the television daily—whether it be on news footage on CNN or HBO's *Shock Video*, and moreover, to be unable to distinguish it from the Hollywood representations of similar occurrences that run simultaneously on adjacent channels. Violence is entertainment, whether it is garnered from religiously following the Gulf War or the *Die Hard* movie sequels. Through disconcerting, hallucinogenic effects that parody television and movies—sometimes seeming like a ride through Universal Studies in Orlando—Stone is able to create for us the same feeling of intoxication that the film industry promotes through the violence-as-entertainment genre.

It is mostly through the character of Wayne Gale (and by the help of Mickey himself) that viewers are reminded of the manufactured (commodified) hyperreality of the media. Gale is the *A Current-Affair* style host of *American Maniacs*. It is through the media coverage they attain from his show that Mickey and Mallory become celebrities—"the best thing to happen to mass murder since Manson." Through Gale's tabloid-style sensationalism, they are transformed into TV icons able to gain enough popularity to appear on the cover of *People* magazine and the same sort of fan appeal that prompted persons to descend upon the Los Angeles County Courthouse with signs to Save O.J. and Free the Juice. Mickey and Mallory's transformation into prime-time stars climaxes in a exclusive interview by Gale broadcast live during halftime of the Super Bowl. And what better moment for the pinnacle of the Mickey and Mallory commodity to be reached than during the yearly entertainment spectacle that epitomizes consumer culture (thirty-second commercial spots during the Super Bowl go for over one million dollars)? Through such depictions as these, Stone dramatizes how media constructions are made and the "shaping effect" on pop-psychology that media images hold.

What viewers finally take away at the conclusion of the movie is the "Evil Demon of Images" that Jean Baudrillard refers to in a book by the same title. The demon—coupled with the predatory wolf—is the dominant metaphor for Mickey that recurs throughout the film. How appropriate they both are for depicting the demonic media itself that parasitically preys on its audience for the fodder that it feeds back to it. As viewers willingly ride along with Mickey and Mallory down Route 666—a TV path(ology) of blood and carnage—into the "final chapter of Mickey and Mallory" the distinction between the TV story and real life suddenly implodes in a crescendo of hyperreality for the viewing audience of the violence-as-entertainment industry (or TV for short) where more and more it seems that *everything* happens for the sake of ratings. And in the closing scene, we watch from "live" remote (along with all the other TV viewers nationwide, as depicted in the movie) as Wayne Gale is made its latest sacrifice.

Notes

INTRODUCTION

1. See McCluhan, Marshall. *Understanding Media*. London: Sphere, 1967.
2. For more, look at Chapter 2 in this book concerning Jean Baudrillard's postmodern denial of Marxism.
3. See Foucault, Michel. *The Order of Things*. Ed. R. D. Laing. New York: Vintage, 1973, for a description of the limits of representation during the classical age and its mutations in the human sciences during the nineteenth century.
4. See Gordon, Avery. *Ghostly Matters*. Minneapolis: University of Minnesota Press, 1997.
5. See Deleuze, Giles. "Plato and the Simulacrum." *The Logic of Sense*. New York: Columbia University Press, 1990. (pp. 253-266).
6. See Jameson, Frederic. "Postmodernism and Consumer Society" *The Anti-Aesthetic*. Ed. Hal Foster. Seattle: Bay Press, 1983.
7. According to Jonathan L. Beller, there is a distinct conversion in "visual economy" from what Walter Benjamin termed aura to what postmodern theory calls "simulacrum." The aura would occur at the moment the eye frames the visual object; simulation follows from the reproduction and high speed circulation of the image of the visual object (e.g., film). The transformation into simulacrum happens as the simulation becomes the substance of circulation receivable at

potentially infinite sites (e.g., in television). In simulacrum, all referentials are liquidated in the field of visual circulation, so that context and conditions of historical production simply no longer matter.

CHAPTER 1

1. See Jean Baudrillard's novel *Cool Memories*. Trans. Chris Turner. New York: Verso, 1990.
2. For text, see "Body Without Organs" by Critical Art Ensemble (first manifestation) in *The Electronic Disturbance*. New York: Autonomedia, 1994. (pp. 71-72).
3. In *Art Papers* (July/August 1997) M.W. Smith writes: "CAE points out that the still-primitive electronic frontier is open to inventors of all types: techno-workers, electronic artists, activists, cyber-critics, etc. . . . What they offer to counter this form of nomadic power is a method of technological decentralization, pressing us to turn from passive consumption to active production in the uses of electronic technologies" (69).

CHAPTER 2

1. See Friedrich Nietzsche's "On Truth and Falsity" or "On Truth and Lie in an Extra-Moral sense" *The Portable Nietzsche*, Ed. Walter Kaufman. New York: Viking, 1954. (pp. 42-47).
2. Here, I am referring specifically to "The System of Objects" and "Consumer Society," in which Jean Baudrillard analyzes consumer objects in terms of code and sets the stage for a formal semiological criticism of Marxism in "For a Critique of the Political Economy of the Sign" and "The Mirror of Production," collected in *Jean Baudrillard: Selected Writings*. Ed. Mark Poster. Stanford: Stanford University Press, 1988.
3. For a more extensive background of Baudrillard's Marxist stage, see *The Mirror of Production*. St. Louis: Telos, 1975.

CHAPTER 4

1. *Nomad* (Editorial), Tallahassee, FL: Spring 1993.

CHAPTER 5

1. See Michel Foucault's discussion of the epochs of language in *The Order of Things*. Ed. R. D. Laing. New York: Vintage, 1973.

CHAPTER 6

1. See Kathy Acker's book of the same title for a postmodern display of symbolic meaning and ritualistic play between sex and death, a self-proclaimed "elegy for the world of the fathers." (*Empire of the Senseless*. New York: Grove Press, 1988.)
2. The Mapplethorpe photo of Acker's defiant face is ripped through the middle.
3. Consider Acker's "Scenes from World War III" in *Wild History*. Ed. Richard Prince. New York: Tanam Press, 1985. (107-116).

CHAPTER 7

1. See hooks, bell, *Yearnings*, p. 28.

CHAPTER 8

1. See Umberto Eco's *Travels in Hyperreality* and Jean Baudrillard's "Astral America" in *Artforum*.
2. See "The Reality Gulf" in *The Guardian*, January 11, 1991: 25, in which Baudrillard predicted that only the simulation of war would occur.

Bibliography

Acker, Kathy. *Blood and Guts in High School*. New York: Grove Press, 1978.
——— *Don Quixote*. New York: Grove Press, 1986.
——— *Empire of the Senseless*. New York: Grove Press, 1988.
——— "Scenes from World War III" in *Wild History*. Ed. Richard Prince. New York: Tanam Press, 1985. (107-116).
Baudrillard, Jean. *America*. New York: Verso, 1988.
——— *Baudrillard Live: Selected Interviews*. Ed. Mike Gane. New York: Routledge, 1993.
——— *Cool Memories*. Trans. Chris Turner. New York: Verso, 1990.
——— "The Ecstasy of Communication." *The Anti-Aesthetic: Essays on Postmodern Culture*. Ed. Hal Foster. Seattle: Bay Press, 1983.
——— *The Ecstasy of Communication*. Ed. Sylvere Lotringer. Trans. Bernard Schutze and Caroline Schutze. New York: Semiotext(e), 1987.
——— *The Evil Demon of Images*. Sydney, Austrailia: Power Institute Publications, 1987.
——— *Fatal Strategies*. Ed. Jim Flemming. Trans. Philip Beitchman and W. G. J. Niesluchowski. New York: Semiotext(e), 1990.
——— *Forget Foucault*. Trans. Nicole Dufresne. New York: Semiotext(e), 1987.
——— *In the Shadow of the Silent Majorities*. New York: Semiotext(e), 1983.
——— *The Mirror of Production*. St. Louis: Telos, 1975.

———*Seduction*. Trans. Brian Singer. New York: St. Martin's, 1990.
———*Selected Writings*. Ed. Mark Poster. Stanford: Stanford University Press, 1988.
———*Simulations*. Trans. Philip Beitchman. New York: Semiotext(e), 1983.
———*Symbolic Exchange and Death*. Trans. Ian Hamilton Grant. London: SAGE, 1993.
Beller, L. Jonathan. "Cinema, Capital of the Twentieth Century." *Postmodern Culture*. 4.3 (May 1994).
Braidotti, Rosi. *Nomadic Subjects*. New York: Columbia University Press, 1994.
Cook, David and Arthur Kroker. *The Postmodern Scene*. New York: St. Martin's, 1986.
Critical Art Ensemble. *The Electronic Disturbance*. New York: Autonomedia, 1994. (PP. 71–72).
Deleuze, Giles. *Neitzsche and Philosophy*. Trans. Hugh Tomlinson. New York: Columbia University Press, 1983.
———"Plato and the Simulacrum." *The Logic of Sense*. New York: Columbia University Press, 1990. (253-266).
Deleuze, Giles and Felix Guattari. *Anti-Oedipus*. Trans. Robert Hurley, Mark Seem, and Helen R. Lane. Minneapolis: University of Minnesota Press, 1983.
———*A Thousand Plateaus*. Trans. Brian Massumi. Minneapolis: University of Minnesota Press, 1987.
DeLillo, Don. *White Noise*. New York: Penguin, 1986.
Denzin, Norman K. *Images of Postmodern Society*. London: Sage Publications, 1991.
Derrida, Jacques. *The Ear of the Other*. Ed. Christie McDonald. Trans. Peggy Kamuf. Lincoln: University of Nebraska Press, 1985.
———*Of Grammatology*. Trans. Gayatri Spivak. Baltimore: Johns Hopkins University Press, 1974.
———*Spurs*. Trans. Barbara Harlow. Chicago: University of Chicago Press, 1979.
Dix, Douglas. "Kathy Acker's Don Quixote: Nomad Writing." *Review of Contemporary Fiction*. 9.3 (Fall 1989): 56-62.
Featherstone, Mike. *Consumer Culture and Postmodernism*. Newbury Park, CA: Sage, 1991.
Foster, Hal. *The Anti-Aesthetic*. Seattle: Bay Press, 1983.
Foucault, Michel. *Language, Counter-memory, Practice*. Ithaca: Cornell University Press, 1977.
———*Madness and Civilization*. Trans. Richard Howard. New York: Vintage, 1965.
———*The Order of Things*. Ed. R. D. Laing. New York: Vintage, 1973.
Gane, Mike. Baudrillard: *Critical and Fatal Theory*. New York: Routledge, 1991.
Gates, Henry Louis. "Beyond the Culture Wars: Identities in Dialogue." *Profession 1993*. New York: MLA, 1993. (6-11).
Gibson, William. *Neuromancer*. New York: Aces Books, 1984.
Gordon, Avery. *Ghostly Matters*. Minneapolis: University of Minnesota Press, 1997.
Harland, Richard. *Superstructuralism*. Ed. Terence Hakes. New York: Metheun, 1987.

Hutcheon, Linda and Joseph Natoli. *A Postmodern Reader*. Albany: State University of New York Press, 1993.

Jameson, Fredric. "Postmodernism and Consumer Society." *Anti-Aesthetic*. Ed. Hal Foster. Seattle: Bay Press, 1983. (111-125).

Jardine, Alice. *Gynesis*. Ithaca: Cornell University Press, 1985.

Kaite, Berkeley. "The Pornographer's Body Double: Transgression Is the Law." *Body Invaders*. Eds. Arthur Kroker and Marilouise Kroker. New York: St. Martin's, 1987. (150-168).

Kellner, Douglas. *Jean Baudrillard. From Marxism to Postmodernism and Beyond*. Cambridge: Polity Press, 1989.

Kristeva, Julia. "Romanticism, Modernism, Postmodernism." *Bucknell Review*. 25.2: 136-141.

Kroker, Arthur. *The Possessed Individual*. Montreal: New World Perspectives, 1992.

———and Charles Levin. "Cynical Power: The Fetishism of the Sign." *Ideology and Power in the Age of Ruins*. Eds. Arthur Kroker and Marilouise Kroker. New York: St. Martin's Press, 1991. (123-134).

———and Marilouise Kroker. *Body Invaders*. New York: St. Martin's, 1987.

Lacan, Jacques. *Ecrits*. Trans. Alan Sheridan. New York: Norton 1977.

Levin, Charles. "Carnal Knowledge of Aesthetic States." *Body Invaders*. Eds. Arthur Kroker and Marilouise Kroker. New York: St. Martin's, 1987. (99-119).

Lowith, Karl. *From Hegel to Nietzsche*. Trans. David Green. New York: Columbia University Press, 1964.

Lyotard, Jean-Francois. *The Postmodern Condition*. Trans. Geoff Bennington and Brian Massumi. Minneapolis: University of Minnesota Press, 1984.

Major, Clarence. *My Amputations*. New York: Fiction Collective, 1986.

Marin, Louis. *Portrait of the King*. Minneapolis: University of Minnesota Press, 1988.

Massumi, Brian. *A User's Guide to Capitalism and Schizophrenia*. Cambridge: Massachusetts Institutte of Technology Press, 1992.

McCaffery, Larry. *After Yesterdays Crash: The Avant-Pop Anthology*. New York: Penguin Books, 1995.

McCluhan, Marshal. *Understanding Media*. London: Sphere, 1967.

McHale, Brian. *Constructing Postmodernism*. New York: Routledge, 1992.

Miller, Lori. "In the Tradition of Cervantes, Sort of." *New York Times Book Review*, November 30, 1986: 10.

Morris, Meaghan. *The Pirate's Fiancée*. New York: Verso, 1988.

Natural Born Killers. Dir. Oliver Stone. Warner Bros., 1994.

Nietzsche, Friedrich. *Beyond Good and Evil*. Trans. R. J. Hollingdale. London: Penguin Books, 1990.

———*The Gay Science*. Trans. Walter Kaufman. New York: Vintage, 1974.

———*The Genealogy of Morals*. Trans. Walter Kaufman and R. J. Hollindale. New York: Vintage, 1969.

———"On Truth and Lie in an Extra-Moral Sense." *The Portable Nietzsche*. Trans. & Ed. Walter Kaufman. New York: Viking, 1954. (42-47).

———*Thus Spoke Zarathustra*. Trans. Walter Kaufman. New York: Viking Penguin, 1966.

———*Twilight of the Idols*. Trans. R. J. Hollingdale. Baltimore: Penguin, 1968.

———*The Will to Power*. Ed. Walter Kaufman. Trans. R. J. Hollingdale and Walter Kaufman. New York: Vintage, 1967.

Norris, Christopher. *What's Wrong with Postmodernism*. Baltimore: John Hopkin's University Press, 1990.

Olalquiaga, Celeste. *Megalopolis*. Minneapolis: University of Minnesota Press, 1992.

Owens, Craig. "The Discourse of Others: Feminists and Postmodernism." *The Anti-Aesthetic*. Ed. Hal Foster. Seattle: Bay Press, 1983. (57-82).

Pfohl, Stephen. *Death at the Parasite Cafe*. New York: St. Martin's, 1992.

Poster, Mark. "Semiology and Critical Theory: From Marx to Baudrillard." *Boundary 2: A Journal of Postmodern Literature and Culture*. 8.1 (Fall 1979): 275-287.

Potter, Russel. "The Hallucination of Textuality." *Nomad*. Tallahassee, FL. #6 (Spring 1994): 23-28.

Pynchon, Thomas. *Vineland*. New York: Penguin, 1990.

Rorty, Richard. *Consequences of Pragmatism*. Minneapolis: University of Minnesota Press, 1982.

———"Feminism and Pragmatism." *Radical Philosophy* (Autumn) (1991): 3-10.

Ross, Andrew. "Baudrillard's Bad Attitude." *Seduction and Theory*. Ed. Dianne Hunter. Chicago: University of Illinois Press, 1989. (214-225).

Singer, Brian. "Baudrillard's Seduction." *Ideology and Power in the Age of Ruins*. Eds. Arthur Kroker and Marilouise Kroker. New York: St. Martin's, 1991. (139-151).

Smith, M. W. "Review: Critical Art Ensemble." *Art Papers*. 21.4 (July/August 1997): 69.

Walsh, Richard. "The Quest for Love and the Writing of Female Desire in Kathy Acker's *Don Quixote*." *Critique: Studies in Contemporary Fiction*. 32.30 (Spring 1991): 149-168.

White, Richard. *Political Theory and Postmodernism*. New York: Cambridge University Press, 1991.

Williams, Reese. *A Pair of Eyes*. New York: Tanam Press, 1983

Zerzan, John. "The Catastrophe of Postmodernism." *Anarchy*. 30 (1991): 16.

Index

A Thousand Plateaus, 7, 74–75
Acker, Kathy, 11, 26, 86, 87, 89, 90, 91, 92, 93, 95, 96; and love, 96–99 *passim*; *Blood and Guts in High School*, 11, 92–97; *Don Quixote*, 11, 85, 87, 95, 96, 98, 99, 100
advertising, 1, 5, 6, 9, 16, 21, 23, 32, 61, 62, 68, 86, 88, 94, 127; as simulacra, 45; codes, 23, 32, 70, 79; industry, 78, 90, 99, 116
America, 1, 113, 115, 116
Anti-Oedipus, 8, 24, 71, 79, 80
appearance, vii, 1, 2, 6, 14, 17, 23, 26, 30–34, 36, 39, 42–51 *passim*, 58, 59, 67, 76, 88, 90, 91, 110, 114–15, 119; pure, 89; strategy of, 89; world of, 87
Appolonian, 36, 40

banal strategies, 48–49
Baudrillard, Jean, vii, viii, 1–4, 6–8, 10, 12, 14–15, 17–20, 22, 23, 25–26, 31–34, 37–38, 57–62, 75–76, 79, 81, 104, 106, 110, 128, 130n, 131n; and Acker, 86–94 *passim*; and America, 113–17 *passim*; "Consumer Society," 33, 130n; "In the Shadow of the Silent Majorities," 52, 69; and seduction, 39–51 *passim*, 65–74; "Simulations," 110; and symbolic exchange, 33, 44–45; *The Ecstasy of Communication*, 45, 68, 89; *The Evil Demon of Images*, 2; "The Mirror of Production," 130n; "The Reality Gulf," 131n; "The System of Objects," 130n; "For a Critique of the Political Economy of the Sign," 59, 130n

becoming, 6–9, 14, 23, 24, 30, 34, 36–37, 42, 47, 70–76 *passim*, 79, 87, 104, 108, 112; -consumer, 7; -molar 8; -other, 9, 12

being, 6, 9, 16, 18, 30, 36, 37, 47, 70, 42, 49, 70, 72, 112–13

Beller, Jonathan, 23, 129n
body, 11, 16, 21, 23, 24, 59, 85–89 *passim;* as object, 89; as text, 86
Braidotti, Rosi, 11, 87
BwO, 7, 8, 24–25, 71–72, 74, 86, 89; as body without organs, 70, 73–74

capitalism, 24, 34–35, 61, 81, 93, 97, 113; late-, 8, 16, 23–24, 52, 59–62 *passim,* 75, 79, 88
capitalist, 9, 24, 59–60, 63, 83, 92, 95; code, 2, 4, 33, 55, 60, 70, 79, 100; commodification, 93, 97; desire, 58, 80, 87; late-, 3–4, 6–7, 20, 23, 26, 59, 78
Cartesian, 15
code, 7–10, 17, 32, 34, 48, 53, 55, 59–60, 67, 70, 86, 89, 123; consumer, 3, 4, 7, 9, 20, 32, 35, 62, 79; electronic, 65; ideological, 35, 80; phallic, 86
coding, 7–9; cultural, 86; system of, 83, 88
commodification, 121, 124
commodity, 4, 7, 8, 23, 33, 55, 59–60, 67, 99, 123–24, 128; corporate, 124; fetishism, 23, 71; form, 57–58, 61–62, 67, 69; identity, 108; image as, 127; sexual, 94; signification, 4; signs, 55
computer, vii, 1, 2, 4, 5, 22–23, 54; model, 55; screen, 68; simulated, 124
conscious, 15, 88; reality, 81
consciousness, 4, 16, 51, 80, 82, 87; collective, 80; false, 67
consumer culture, 4, 26, 60, 114, 120
consumerism, 8, 10, 55, 66, 119
consumption, 3–4, 6–7, 9, 33–34, 44, 60–62, 66, 68, 71, 123; of signs, 60–61, 86
Cook, David, 4–5, 10–12, 16
Critical Art Ensemble, 22, 24–26, 72, 86, 130n; *The Electronic Disturbance,* 130n
cybernetic, 18, 21–24, 52, 70; space, 66, 68
cyberspace, 21, 24, 70

Debord, Guy, 23, 59
Deleuze, Giles, viii, 6–8, 12, 16–17, 24, 26, 51, 65, 70–75 *passim,* 87, 93, 104, 129n
Deleuzian, 24, 79, 87
DeLillo, Don, 116; *White Noise,* 116
Denzin, Norman, 11, 59
Derrida, Jacques, 4, 6, 16, 31, 46, 79; *Spurs,* 46
Descartes, Rene, 15–16
desert, 114–19 *passim*
desire, 6–7, 9, 11–12, 15, 49, 51, 58–59, 61–62, 71, 86–89 *passim,* 92–93, 99; as production, 7, 59, 71; order of, 89
desiring machines, 7, 23, 71, 72, 74
deterritorialization, 7, 14, 24, 73, 76, 94
deterritorialize, 10, 12, 71, 74, 80, 86
Dewey, John, 17–19 *passim*
difference, 6, 8–9, 12, 14, 35–36, 39, 42, 47, 50, 56, 71–72, 89, 105, 115, 117
Disneyland, 113–14
Dix, Douglas, 87, 99, 100
DNA, vii, 18, 35, 55, 121; evidence, 124; model, 65
double, 14, 16, 30, 34–36, 47, 56, 61, 67, 69, 93
Dyonesian, 36, 40

Eco, Umberto, 113, 131
ecstasy, 35, 67, 69, 90; of communication, 69
Ellison, Ralph, 110; *The Invisible Man,* 108–11 *passim*
enchantment, 46, 91, 97, 101
Enlightenment, 4, 13, 15, 31, 35, 38; dream, 43; philosophy, 38, 49

fashion, 1, 6, 32, 49, 55, 62, 66, 86, 88–89, 90; as industry, 93–94, 96, 116
fatal strategies, 4, 6, 10, 18, 34–35, 37–38, 43, 48–49, 62, 89, 115
Featherstone, Mike, 59, 78
feminine, 46–47, 49, 87–89, 92; identity, 96, 99–100

INDEX

Foucault, Michel, 4, 13–14, 16–19, 21, 27, 78–79, 129n–30n; and power, 52–55; *The History Of Sexuality*, 53; *The Order of Things*, 129n–30n
Freud, Sigmund, 15
Freudianism, 34

Gane, Mike, 4, 31, 38–39, 45, 48, 60, 88, 90
Gates, Henry, 104
Gibson, William, 18, 68; *Neuromancer*, 18, 68
God, 4, 13, 16–17, 29, 50–51
Gordon, Avery, 129n; *Ghostly Matters*, 129n
Guattari, Felix, 6–8, 12, 17, 24, 26, 51, 65, 71–75, 87, 93, 104
Gulf War, 2, 49, 54, 62, 120–21, 127–28; as hyperreal, 114

Habermas, Jurgen, 17
Hegel, G.W.F., 14
Heidegger, Martin, 75
history, 3, 5–6, 10, 14, 67, 69, 71, 77–78; and America, 113–14; tv, 116–17
Husserl, Edmund, 16
Hutcheon, Linda, 3; *A Postmodern Reader*, 3
hyperreal, 1–2, 5, 8, 32–33, 37–39, 42–45, 49–50, 56–57, 59, 62, 86, 90, 106, 113–15, 127; author, 111; culture, 5; dimension, 88; O.J., 119–24 *passim*; war, 127. *See also* simulacra
Hyperreality, 1, 3, 10, 17, 32, 38, 43, 45, 49–52, 54–57, 67–68, 70, 78, 114, 116; and *Natural Born Killers*, 125–27; of the media, 128

identity, 6, 10, 12, 23, 24, 59, 70–71, 75, 79–80, 86–87, 91, 93, 99, 103, 105–7, 109, 111; black, 108, 111; cultural, 104–5; made commodity, 11; masks of, 106; mythical, 106

illusion, 42–45, 47–51, 69, 79, 90, 94; of the real, 67; of the sign, 92
image, 4–6, 9–10, 15–17, 20–23, 32, 34, 42, 45, 57, 81–82, 88, 122–23; as commodity, 3–4, 34, 59, 61; consumption, 9; processing, 77; production, 58
images, 1–3, 4, 6, 8–9, 11–12, 14, 16, 19, 21, 26, 30, 42–43, 50–51, 54–56, 59, 61–62, 70, 71, 75, 78–79, 81–83, 86–87, 92–93, 119, 122–23, 126; lifestyle, 11; reprocessed, 78
implosion, 5–6, 8, 12, 38–39, 42–43, 54, 117; of meaning, 8, 10, 26, 69
individual, 4, 11, 14–15, 17–25 *passim*, 32, 68, 79–80, 82
information, 6, 13, 20–21, 23, 32, 48, 49, 54, 65, 69, 71; coding, 55; society, 71

Jameson, Fredric, 5, 23, 77, 82, 111, 129n; "Postmodernism and Consumer Society," 77, 129n
Jardine, Alice, 20, 78
JFK, 54, 78, 121

Kellner, Douglas, 20, 49, 55, 76
King, Rodney, 49–50, 123, 127
knowledge, 13–14, 18–22 *passim*, 26–27, 37, 90
Kristeva, Julia, 77
Kroker, Arthur, 4, 5, 8–12, 15–16, 18, 21, 36–37, 39, 43, 51, 53–57, 60, 62, 66–68, 71, 73, 75, 86, 93; *Body Invaders*, 86; *Panic Encyclopedia*, 10; *The Possessed Individual*, 4; *The Postmodern Scene*, 4, 10
Kroker, Marilouise, 10
Kruger, Barbara, 9, 62

Lacan, Jacques, 15, 30, 61, 77, 81
Lacanian, 110
Levin, Charles, 81
lines of flight, 7–8, 12, 73–74, 76, 80, 89, 94, 100, 112

Lyotard, Jean-Francois, 16-17, 19, 20, 23

Major, Clarence, 11, 103, 106-12 passim; *My Amputations*, 11, 103, 104, 106, 108, 112
Man, 14-20 passim; 29, 39, 78, 81
Marin, Robert, 5; *Portrait of the King*, 5
Marxism, 4, 75
Marxist, 3, 15, 33
masculine, 47, 49, 87, 89, 91-93, 96-97; authority, 89; culture, 96; desire, 88-93 passim; identity, 97; myth, 91; order, 90, 92, 97-98, 100; will, 91
masks, 103, 105-12 passim
Massumi, Brian, 7-10, 86-87
McCaffery, Larry, 119; *After Yesterday's Crash: The Avant-Pop Anthology*, 119
McCluhan, Marshal, 68, 129n; *Understanding Media*, 129n
media, 2, 5, 8-12, 18, 20-21, 26, 33-34, 42, 49, 50-52, 53-55, 61-62, 69, 86, 88, 103, 116, 120, 122, 126-28; culture, 12, 19; image, 120, 128; mass, 5-6, 32, 83, 119; representations, 105, 120; scene, 66
models, 2, 13, 18, 21, 32, 34, 37, 43, 45, 55-56; sexual, 88; technological, 18
molar, 71, 75; identity, 103; individual, 104; men, 87; versus molecular, 104
molecular, 71, 75; lines of flight, 73
Montrelay, Michele, 46
Morris, Meaghan, 14
Morrison, Toni, 108

Natoli, Joseph, 3; *A Postmodern Reader*, 3
Natural Born Killers, 12, 120, 125-27 passim
Nietzsche, 4-6, 9-19 passim, 26, 35-46 passim, 50-51, 55, 59, 62, 66, 67, 72-76, 105, 110, 127, 130n; *The Gay Science*, 4, 29; *The Geneology of Morals*, 75; on "the will," 9, 29, 32, 35-36, 62, 75, 91; on "truth," 29-32; "On Truth and Lie in the Extra-Moral Sense," 130n; *The Will To Power*, 5, 13, 29, 36, 75; *Thus Spoke Zarathustra*, 6, 30; *Twilight of the Idols*, 36
Nietzschean, 8, 12, 18, 31, 38-39, 46-47, 68, 71, 74, 79
nihilism, 4, 10, 13, 16, 30, 36-40, 44-45, 57, 59, 61, 63, 70, 72, 75-76, 96, 127; postmodern, 4, 39, 47
nihilistic, 11, 13, 16, 30, 35-36, 51, 62, 72, 74; logic, 40; power, 47; simulation, 39; subject, 106; thought, 35; will, 36-37, 47, 75
Norris, Christopher, 3, 32, 38, 44
nomad, 80, 100
nomadic, 6, 11, 24, 80, 87; mode, 86; subjectivity, 79; transformation, 87

object, 6-8, 14, 18, 22-23, 30, 32, 38-39, 42, 45, 47-48, 59, 61-62, 74, 79, 88-89, 91, 94; logic of, 7; resistance as, 7
objectivity, 18, 37, 39
obscene, 23, 47-48, 50, 54, 61, 69, 90-92, 95, 115; gesture, 69
obscenity, 10, 23, 33, 47-48, 50, 54, 65, 69, 90, 94, 125; of the image, 113; radical, 44
Olalquiaga, Celeste, 23, 60, 70
Orwell, George, 21; *1984*, 21
Other, 11, 15, 17, 22, 79-80, 97, 103, 107
otherness, 17

perspectival, 5, 12, 26, 36, 62, 74; appearances, 15, 30, 36, 55, 65-66; illusion, 5, 31, 48; space, 37, 42, 52, 58, 66, 79; truth effects, 31; will, 41; world, 36
Pfohl, Stephen, 2, 10, 21, 24-25, 45, 53, 66, 75; *Death at the Parasite Café*, 10
phallocentric, 11, 91, 94, 96; logic, 99; order, 95, 101; text, 11, 85-86 99; vision, 11
phallogocentrism, 47, 85
Plato, 5, 35
Platonic, 35

pornographic, 25, 70, 90–91, 116; culture, 90; image, 92, 116; language, 99; object, 93–94
pornography, 48, 88–90, 92, 94–95, 125
Poster, Mark, 33
postmodern, vii, viii, 3-6, 8-21 *passim*, 24, 26-27, 31, 35-39, 41–42, 47, 54, 59, 61, 74, 83, 87, 96, 111, 116; abyss, 124; age, 36; condition, 11, 53, 79, 110, 113; critic, 78; culture, 4, 17, 35, 39, 52, 57-58, 62, 78, 103; desire, 75; experience, 39, 63, 66, 75; humans, 18; individual, 20, 62; object, 12, 113; power, 10, 53; scene, 27; self, 11, 82; simulacra, 2, 8, 13; society, 19, 21, 53, 55, 69; subjects, 10, 24, 62, 66-67, 71, 78, 104; will, 9, 37; world, 38, 50, 71, 75, 79; writing, 10, 26
postmodernism, viii, 3, 16, 31, 38, 51, 77–78
postmodernity, 1, 4, 6, 8, 10, 17, 19, 29, 47, 54, 58, 75, 86, 106–7, 110, 117
poststructural, 16, 79; sign–slide, 75
power, 4, 5, 10, 15, 17–19, 21, 23, 26, 47, 49, 87–88; and Foucault, 52–54; cynical, 52, 74; of the feminine, 47; of seduction, 88, 90
production, 9–10, 44, 58–59, 62, 66, 71–72, 74, 89–90; of desire, 6, 67, 75, 80; of images, 86; of meaning, 76, 78; of simulacra, 75; social, 72
psychoanalysis, 72, 88
Pynchon, Thomas, 2, 18, 116; *Vineland*, 2, 18, 116

rape, 98, 126
rationalism, 43; ideal of, 87
reproduced, 42, 106, 112
reproduction, 42, 56, 60, 112; of capital, 88; of images, 16
reading, vii, viii, 6, 10, 12, 80; subject, 77, 82
real, vii, 2–6, 15, 23, 25–26, 32–39 *passim*, 42–43, 48–50, 54–56, 60, 62, 66, 69, 75, 104, 109–10, 114, 116, 120, 122, 124, 126–27
reality, vii, viii, 1–5, 7, 10, 16–20, 30–32, 42–45, 50–57 *passim*, 69, 72, 78, 91, 104, 127
representation, viii, 2–4, 6, 13–15, 17, 23, 26, 31–32, 40, 45, 50, 52, 56, 66, 72–73, 78, 112, 116–17, 122; false, 46
representational, 4–5, 15, 17, 19–20, 51, 88; codes and images, 90; desire, 90; doublings, 75; power, 5, 53; space, 52; thought, 4
rhizomatic, 7–8, 26, 72, 74–75, 94; becoming, 8; deterritorialization, 72–73; existence, 71; form, 76; lines of flight, 83; maneuvering, 79, 94; production, 73
rhizomes, 73
Rorty, Richard, 17, 26, 31
Ross, Andrew, 115
rupture, 7–8, 11–12, 73, 80, 82, 86

de Saussure, Ferdinand, 16
Saussurian, 33, 78
schizo, 50–51, 71–72; living, 74
schizoanalysis, 71, 74
schizoid, 7, 12, 71, 75, 80; behavior, 12; discourse, 79–80; ethics, 83; sign, 11; subject, 71–72; text, 79
schizophrenia, 6–8, 12, 104; cultural, 6–7, 78
schizophrenic, 7–8, 24, 26, 50, 69–71, 74–75, 78–79, 81-82
Schopenhauer, Arthur, 15
screen, 20–25, 42, 45, 47–48, 50, 52, 53, 58, 61, 70, 72, 81–82, 120, 124
screenal, 2, 23, 25, 62, 69, 113; body, 22; culture, 33, 81; image, 20, 24, 48, 124; space, 25
seduction, 6–8, 12, 14, 22, 25–26, 38–40, 58–61, 65, 67–68, 72–73, 75–76, 86–92, 115–16, 119; and the feminine, 44–51 *passim*
seductive, 5, 37, 39, 46, 51, 62, 66, 89; attraction, 44; strategy, 92
self, 10–11, 15–17, 21–22, 30, 35, 61, 65, 70, 72, 74, 79, 81, 88, 95, 99,

104–8; authentic, 81, 106; postmodern, 59; virtual, 70, 94
semiurgical, 4, 14, 60, 89, 106
semiurgy, 21, 24, 43; radical, 4, 52
sex, 18, 68, 87–88, 90–93, 126
sexual, 11, 48, 88, 90, 95, 98; acts, 90; desire, 65, 90, 96, 98; difference, 88; exchange, 96, 98; exploitation, 95; love, 97; object, 93; violence, 95
sexuality, 11, 53, 59, 86–89, 92–94, 97, 98-99
sign(s), 1, 4, 6–8, 10, 16, 17, 19–20, 23, 26, 30, 32, 34, 36–38, 42–44, 54–60 *passim*, 67, 76, 78, 80–81, 83, 86, 89–92, 110, 116–17, 119, 123; cynical, 10, 51, 55, 58, 60, 66, 68–69, 72, 74, 76; image, 7, 16; logic of, 5, 60, 81; of desire, 86, 91; postmodern, 6, 115; production, 58, 60; political economy of, 86; paranoic, 72; ritual, 76
Simpson, O.J., 2, 12, 25, 43, 52, 62, 119–28 *passim*
simulacra, viii, 1–2, 5–8, 10–12, 15–18, 21, 32–35, 37–38, 42, 52, 56–57, 58, 62, 67–68, 72–73, 75, 78, 82–83, 96, 98–100, 103, 105, 107–8, 110–12, 114. *See also* hyperreal
simulacrum, vii, 2–3, 6–7, 9, 11–12, 24–25, 31–32, 33–36, 38, 40, 46–49, 51–53, 56–57, 61–62, 66–67, 70–71, 73, 76, 78, 85, 88, 91, 103–5, 110, 113–15, 119; cultural, 11; logic of, 3; technological, 86
simulated, vii, 6, 18, 26, 32, 37–39, 53–54, 57–59, 91; consensus, 6; desire, 61, 87; experience, 32; identity, 61; models, 44, 58, 62; order, 55; space, 39, 52, 70; will, 45; world, 66; violence, 50
simulation, vii, viii, 1–3, 5–10, 14, 20–22, 24, 26, 27, 30, 32, 34–35, 37–60 *passim*, 62, 65, 67, 74–75, 78, 88–92, 106, 108, 110, 113, 115–17; models, 69
Singer, Brian, 43, 51, 57
Smith, M.W., 130n

Stone, Oliver, 12, 125–26
subject, 7, 9, 14, 16–18, 20, 26, 30, 39, 48–49, 53, 61, 70, 75, 78–80, 94
subjectivity, viii, 3–8, 10–11, 18, 20–22, 24, 31, 41, 49, 52, 60–61, 65–69, 72–74, 80, 82, 87; autonomous, 106; female, 86; modern, 20; postmodern, 66

technological, 18–19, 21, 23–24, 26, 51; body, 23; culture, 67; images, 54, 67; nihilism, 67; society, 69
technology, vii, 9, 11, 13, 17, 19–20, 26–27, 29, 34, 55, 67–68, 71–72, 80, 86
television, 1–2, 12, 18, 25–26, 31, 35, 42, 45, 48–49, 52, 55, 57, 62, 66, 68, 71, 80, 90, 93, 120, 128. *See also* tv
truth, 2, 4, 10, 13, 15, 18, 26, 29–31, 35–36, 39, 44, 46–48, 50–51, 72, 89–90; of appearance, 31
tv, 2, 18, 20–22, 25, 32, 43, 45, 50–52, 57, 59, 61–62, 66, 86, 90, 96, 104–5, 113–14, 116, 120–24, 126–28. *See also* television
Tzu, Lao, 81

unconscious, 15, 81; desire, 88

virtual, 2, 18–21, 25, 62, 70; body, 70, 86; dimension, 10; feminism, 94; imagery, 68; mediascape, 72; reality, 68, 94; power, 68; world, 25, 66–67

Walsh, Richard, 95
will to power, 5, 18, 21, 29, 36–37, 40, 51, 53, 58, 62, 74–76, 91, 105
will to will, 9, 26, 35–36, 50, 59, 62, 67
Williams, Reese, 11, 26, 78, 80–83; *A Pair of Eyes*, 11, 78–83 *passim*
woman, 46, 87, 91
Wright, Richard, 105, 108, 111; *Native Son*, 108, 111